The
Transforming
MIND

A. 85

The Transforming Mind

Laurence Bendit and Phoebe Bendit

*This publication made possible with
the assistance of the Kern Foundation*

The Theosophical Publishing House
Wheaton, Ill. U.S.A.
Madras, India / London, England

Library of Congress Catalog Number: 74-103415
ISBN: 0-8356-0012-2

Printed in the United States of America.

An animal is a passive creature; it adapts to its environment. Man became an evolutionary force when he overcame the "passive fallacy" that governs the animal's attitude, when he discovered that his efforts could change the world. A human being is a creature who has made Mr. Polly's discovery: "If you don't like your life, you can change it." Man has reached an impasse in his evolutionary development because he has not yet made the discovery that his perception can also be changed; where consciousness is concerned, he still suffers from the "passive fallacy" — that as things are, so they must remain.

Colin Wilson, *Introduction to the New Existentialism*

The true conqueror is he
Who is not conquered
By the multitude of the small.
The mind is this conqueror —
But only the mind
Of the wise man.

Chuang Tzu

CONTENTS

FOREWORD

Some books are the products of their time, reflecting attitudes, patterns of thought, philosophic views contemporary with the period in which they are brought to birth in published form. Absorbing and challenging they may be, but such books are mirrors. There are other books, however, which constitute windows, and as such they are less products of their time than forecasters of a future. For they open the mind and heart to vistas of what yet may be, the promise of tomorrow.

The present work, by that remarkable husband-and-wife team Laurence and Phoebe Bendit, is the second kind of book, one that provides encouragement as well as guidance for the adventurer into the realm of the mind in search of its transformative possibilities. Though largely a product of the early 1960s (when Dr. and Mrs. Bendit were resident in California involved in the reestablishment of the Krotona Institute School of Theosophy) the book does not so much address the turbulence and uncertainties of that decade. Rather it points beyond the muddled scene of an era that seemed to lay waste the cherished values of our human heritage to a "beyond-world," as the authors call it. They envisioned a world in which a reconciliation of all opposites can take place by and through the awakening advance of human consciousness itself. In that sense, the book is even more relevant today, in the 1980s, when we realize that time may still run out for the human venture unless we act responsibly and from knowledge of that deeper center, the "Essential Self," grounded in the Universal. The choice indeed is *ours!*

Who were the Bendits? Their contributions to theosophical literature were considerable, although less in bulk than that of some other writers within the Theosophical Movement. Their effectiveness must be measured, not by the number of books written, but in the seminal ideas given expression and in the creative interplay of those ideas as they flowed from two very original thinkers. Phoebe Payne Bendit was a natural clairvoyant for whom life always showed the dual face of physical and psychical reality within a simultaneity of appearance. She disciplined her psychic perceptivity through a study of psychology in order to utilize her talents in therapy, particularly with disturbed children. Laurence John Bendit was a trained psychiatrist, with degrees (M.A., M.D., and B. Chir.) from Cambridge University; a specialist in psychological medicine, he studied under Dr. Carl Jung, as did his wife, Phoebe. Together, both in psychological and therapeutic practice and in teaching and lecturing for the Theosophical Society, they constituted a unique team, collaborating in writing and in that deeper continuing search for understanding which so marks their books as less summaries of arrived-at conclusions than insightful questionings into whatever might lie beyond.

One of the last, if not the last of their joint endeavors to be published is *The Transforming Mind,* and this writer, at least, must express gratitude to The Theosophical Publishing House of Wheaton for bringing it into print again. It speaks of "the austerity of the real search" as we move toward that consciousness of our shared destiny in One World. At a time of get-psychic-quick schemes, of lazy minds abandoning themselves to the latest guru who promises salvation, this work reminds the genuine aspirant of "the vital importance of the mind of man, not only to himself but to the whole planet, at every level," but they speak of a mind rooted in compassion, embracing universals, moving always beyond itself. For our need — and it is an even more urgent need today than when this book first appeared over a decade ago — is "for progressive change and reorganization of our world outlook." In these days the only worldview that will suffice is one that can comprehend our unique and individual responsibility in creating our own future through the transforming potential of consciousness. Such a worldview is theosophic, rooted in an interior Wisdom; it is the natural concomitant of a mind that has come truly awake (as the Buddha was awake, since *budh* means simply to be awake) to its own possibilities, never content with the "as is," but forever seeking the Vision Splendid of an enlightened humanity.

One final word: I am certain Laurence and Phoebe would have recognized the principle of synchronicity at work in the simple fact that this book was germinated during their tenure at the Krotona Institute School of Theosophy, where the foreword for this reprinting is being written. The Ojai Valley was once recognized by that remarkable visionary and practical leader Dr. Annie Besant as a site where the future could indeed come to birth. It is uniquely fertile soil for the growth of minds, of consciousnesses, committed not only to their own transformation, but to the transformation and redemption of the world. Synchronicity or not, the world has need of consciousness forever willing to grow beyond itself in its search for truth. This book can provide, for those who take its message to heart, the fertilizing ingredients for just such a transformation.

JOY MILLS
Director, Krotona School
of Theosophy

PREFACE

When our friends, having got wind of the fact that we were writing a book, asked us, "What is it about this time?" we found it difficult to explain in a few words. If we were rash enough to use such a word as *existential* or *existence* most of them would at once say, "I have never understood what existentialism is all about," whereupon further discussion followed, particularly on the matter of the difference between existentialism and an existential attitude. One of our purposes, therefore, is to try and clarify certain ideas and to propose some basic principles out of which a practical way of life for ordinary people might be developed, each one for himself, and on his own unique pattern. The first part of this book tries to do the first, the second to see how the principles apply in various fields. It might be put that the earlier part states the theme; the second consists of variations on this; and the whole is followed by a coda.

Needless to say, we shun dogmatism of any kind and at any level. If we say a thing affirmatively it is simply to avoid the tedious qualification which would be needed on every page. The whole book may be said to be written under a heading, writ large, *"It seems as if . . . ."* We are today getting past the age of certainty, of saying, in the way of old-fashioned theologians and scientists alike, "This is so and forever shall be." *Panta rhei,* "all is in flux," is even more cogent today than when Heraclitus of Ephesus said it twenty-five centuries ago.

What kind of book is this, then? Let it be said clearly and immediately, it is not a scientific treatise. Science, however immensely valuable, and however much its frontiers are widening, is a limited discipline, and understanding of man cannot be fitted into a scientific framework. Medicine has always been called an art as well as a science, and the art is essential to good practice. But even then, as Kenneth Walker and his fellow surgeon Alexis Carrel realized, "the mystery remains." Man cannot be enclosed by science; rather is science enclosed within the wider human mind.

Is it then a book on religion? Not in any academic sense. Though we constantly refer to God, the Essence, the Numen or Noumenon, Tao, using such terms interchangeably, we do so only in an attempt to separate basic Religion from more mundane conceptions of it. Moreover, by bringing together elements from different philosophies, particularly the Vedantist, Buddhist and Taoist schools, with here and there a touch of Zen, and by linking them together with Christian concepts, it then becomes possible to extricate the latter from the prison of what has been called "churchianity" and the accumulation of doctrines which are not to be found in the Gospels. In this way it can be shown that what we call Christianity existed long before the beginning of our era, in remote parts of the world, where the name of Jesus had never been heard; and hence we hope to point out its universal validity, for all time and in all forms of religion, under whatever label it was presented.

Nor is this a book on psychology, despite frequent reference to Freud and Jung, particularly the latter. Pyschology can become a barrier to untrammeled insight, when it has once served its purpose in dealing with individual problems.

At that we had better leave it, hoping that if we have clarified nothing, we shall at least not have added to the confusion of thought today. We have, moreover, carefully skirted round some subjects, such as dream analysis, which have already been amply discussed elsewhere.

One of our difficulties has been to find language for some of our ideas. Here, while keeping technical or unusual words to a minimum we have unashamedly borrowed others. But the way we have applied terms and concepts is almost sure to offend some scholars and semantic experts. What were we to do? And does it follow that if our idea of, for instance, that vexed word "existence" differs from that of others, we are of necessity wrong?

We do not claim originality for what we have written. On the contrary, we gratefully acknowledge our debts to such people as J. Krishnamurti and H. P. Blavatsky; Paul Tillich, the modern and Protestant theologian, and Pierre Teilhard de Chardin, the Jesuit paleontologist; Freud and Jung; and to the very many others from whom we have learned even if they did not know that they were teaching us.

Finally, if the essays of which this book consists do not seem to be consecutive, developing a certain theory and reaching a conclusion, this is partly from necessity, partly because we feel it desirable to remain inconclusive.

The necessity lies in the fact that though there are all kinds of would-be conclusive ideas about man and his development, none of them really meets the case. They start from certain fixed premises and try to turn these into an all-embracing system. We feel, however, that it is better to use the map-makers' principle, taking sights from different points and so building up a triangulated map in general terms, without filling in the details of the ground between. In this way anybody who wants to can use these points and yet choose his route from one to the other, so making his own explorations and gaining his own experience.

There is also a reason for considering conclusiveness as positively undesirable. In our view, to conclude is to kill. The very word comes from the Latin *claudere,* to close, shut or confine. No plant other than molds, fungi or other forms of life associated with decay will grow in a closed vessel. Life will not be confined; it vanishes when anything is concluded at the mental as much as at the physical level; and now is the time when more than at any other we need fresh growth and forward movement if we are not to be caught in the toils of any fixed system, be it Christian, Marxist, scientific or what have you.

Further, an *unsatisfied* mind bears in it the urge to go on groping, and so growing. It is alive, and quite different from a *dissatisfied* one; for the latter likes its ideas neatly sealed into well wrapped packages and is unhappy when they are labile and mutable. So it is part of a deliberate purpose, as well as fulfilling the needs of a situation where we are trying to forecast the future, to suggest rather than state unequivocally what seems to be the line of development today.

Our special thanks are due to Mrs. Joyce Beavis for her careful reading and shrewd comments on our MS, and to Mrs. Jane Hammond for providing us with a tidy version of what was a very rough draft, full of corrections.

L.J.B.
P.D.B.
Pembury, Tunbridge Wells, England, 1967-8

PART I

Chapter I

INTRODUCTION

It may seem trite to start this book by pointing a finger at the peril in which mankind stands today, but there is a reason for doing so, in that until we discover the real roots of the danger it will tend to hang over us as a constant menace. In this case we are inclined to look only at the obvious: the threat of nuclear war; and, if we are of that temperament, of communism or capitalism or any other ideology, such as Catholicism or Protestantism, religion or irreligion, and say that here is the basis of our present state. In reality, however, these are only symptoms of the disease which originates deeper than this. It springs from the human mind which is mother to them all.

This mind has produced weapons which, however, unless misused because of an act of that mind, are entirely innocent and harmless in themselves. It has elaborated the systems from which ideologies and religious dogmas have emerged. And, above all, it has interfered with the slow, plodding rhythms of Nature and so changed, and is changing, the whole face of creation, at least in our corner of the universe.

If we imagine the world in its beginning, before man as we know him today peopled it to any extent, we can see it as going its own way, evolving new species, eliminating many, and taking endless time over it. Man seems unnecessary to the process, at any rate as an independent species. This, however, if modern scientists are to be believed, is a misconception. For, it seems, physical evolution appears to have ground almost to a standstill after producing the anthropoid apes. There has been no new development in terms of organs for many millennia. But, it is pointed out, the process has continued in another sphere. Using a somewhat mediocre animal body, the key has moved up the scale and now operates not in the physical structure but in the mental; man, the thinking animal, predominates, and it is through him that evolution not only proceeds but succeeds in breaking new ground, producing things which, without man, would never be. It is almost infinitely improbable that — whether the universe is the better for them or not — such things as, say, nylon, jet engines, books and a myriad other commonplace things in use today would ever have been created.

This is on the constructive side, and marvelous it is. But we have reached the point where we are brought face to face with the fact that we have it in our power to sterilize the earth and reduce it to a moon-like lump of ash. If this happened, the evolutionary process would be stopped, or would have to begin all over again. Perhaps even the mineral earth would suffer, lacking the animal and vegetable waste out of which come chalky rocks and the reputedly mineral oils, coal and so on, which form a considerable proportion of the globe. Mankind has received a shock. Leaving aside the rights and wrongs of the Hiroshima bomb, we have actually seen on a small scale what could happen on a large one, and this has hastened our realization that we must change or die. Mankind is still at the stage where the carrot and the goad, at opposite ends, are needed for the majority of us. Our minds have been developed on this pattern, as we shall presently explain.

Now, however, a change is needed, all the more revolutionary in that it demands a complete alteration of values. This should not be based on a sense of guilt, of "original sin," but on a *metanoia*, a "knowing again" such as is advocated in the Gospels. Sins there will always be until man reaches perfection. But almost all sin is in reality merely mistake, not deliberate wrong-doing, and is based on ignorance or only partial knowledge, and lack of imagination. It is not eliminated by moral exhortation: we have heard this for millennia from preachers and prophets, and the results are, on the whole, very poor. But there is another way, in tune with the mood of today. The way through the present crisis, is to learn to understand ourselves. It was clearly advocated at Delphi for those who wanted to understand the Oracle, which, in effect, would present

2

them with a cryptic message from their inner being. The Delphic advice was pithily echoed by Alexander Pope in the eighteenth century of our era, when he wrote:

> .... Know thyself, presume not God to scan.
>   The proper study of Mankind is man,
>   Placed on this isthmus of a middle state,
>   A being darkly wise and rudely great,
>   With too much knowledge for the sceptic side.
>   With too much weakness for the stoic's pride ...

Krishnamurti says the same today, and indeed many thinking people realize the truth, that only as we know ourselves can we bring about the inner transformation which will lead to a real and deep re-ordering of the world.

Pope, perhaps without realizing it, went very deep into the nature of man when he spoke of him as "on an isthmus of a middle state." What lies on each side and at each end of the strip of land? To be in a "middle state" indicates that man is between two extremes. Nietzsche, more dramatically, sees man as on a tight-rope over an abyss, with peril on each side; peril in trying to go back on his steps; peril in moving forward; peril in standing still. The idea is the same: man is a transitionary product of the total stretch of evolution. He is *on* the evolutionary track, not *outside* it; but he is in a special place on it, one where the emphasis changes, and where the resolution of that change has to be self-induced, not left to the forces of Nature alone. Left to herself, Nature would doubtless go on with her slow, regular cycles. With the intervention of her own product, man, the cycles are apt to be broken, and the whole balance of life is affected. It may be questioned whether, if this did not occur, things could go on otherwise than in a stereotyped manner, leading nowhere. With man entering the scheme, it becomes possible to envisage the emergence of something else, a new pattern in Nature herself, perhaps, such as we cannot really yet conceive. In any case, man is capable of bringing about a new order of life on the earth — or equally, of abolishing even what is already there.

He is on an isthmus, too, in that he not only lies between the two mainland kingdoms of prehumanity and posthumanity, he is in a perilous position if he strays too far on either side. If he should lose sight of the axis of the isthmus, he will fall into oblivion, probably taking the rest of live creation with him. He is therefore in the position where he must try to tread the middle of a narrow causeway running between what has been and what can be, in order to link the two. No other creature in our part of the universe appears capable of doing this. Hence the importance of setting a proper course.

That course, however, like that of any tongue of land between continents is not of necessity straight. On the contrary, in the case of evolution, it appears to be curved, to follow a spiral track, returning over itself time and time again, yet with a difference at each turn due to the passage of time if to nothing else. Hence, if man goes straight on from where he stands now, he will find himself off course and, as we have said, falling into an abyss. On the other hand, if he changes too abruptly, the same thing will happen. He needs to find the progressive line which will keep him at the right distance from the center of the spiral yet constantly related to it. We shall discuss the nature of the center as we go further into the subject. But clearly, without it there would be no spiral, so its importance is paramount.

Before we come to this, however, it may be useful if we take a general view of the evolutionary process which leads up to man and demands of him certain things.

If we take a long view, and even if we choose to ignore Teilhard de Chardin's religious background, it is evident that forward evolutionary movement, whatever its physical manifestations, is accompanied by a process at another level. We may call this "life energy" or what we will, but in any case it shows us an uninterrupted stream running from preconscious mechanical reactions toward instinctive behavior. Hence arise, first, consciousness as we understand it, and later, self-consciousness. The latter, to quote Teilhard de Chardin, is not only to know, but to know oneself as knowing.

In the earlier stages — the mineral — the response, if it can be called this, is entirely to stimuli coming from outside. Gravity, heat, forces of all kinds affect the mineral which "responds" by showing certain qualities which we call mass, inertia, a re-arrange-ment of atoms and molecules which alter its physical character. We see here something which precedes perception and the action-producing aspect of mind which is technically known as conation. Mineral reactions are consistent, blind, and entirely automatic.

In the vegetable stage we find the same characteristics, but they are absorbed and adapted into a more elaborate system. Biochemistry is chemistry, but it centers round a few chemical elements only; others play a subsidiary role. It is principally concerned with very large molecules with peculiar properties, which, like the nucleic acids and the enzymes, are associated with what we call life. This makes the plant the first *organic* entity, capable of self-reproduction and reduplication, and of a measure of adaptability to external conditions. This adaptation may be immediate, or work in a wider field through mutation.

The animal kingdom starts at much the same point as the plant, in single-celled, self-reproducing protozoa. These enclose the vegetative functions in a further state, where the power to move about is the prime obvious difference. This leads to simple nervous reflex actions, conditioned reflexes — the root of learning — and hence to instinct which is passed on from animal to animal in some mysterious manner. This occurs perhaps through the group of proteins connected with physical genetics; it is itself *unlearned* by each single beast. The behavior of an animal hunting its prey is a long way from the reactions of minerals to external impacts, yet it can be seen as being on the same strand of evolution as that which eventually leads to the development of mind. At this point, external events no longer always produce immediate reactions. Factors emanating from within the animal play into the pattern and often modify the result. The totality of these inner factors, we label mind or psyche.

Mind may thus be said to originate together with the power to choose and judge, and hence to vary response to instinctive mandates. A primitive animal like the amoeba encounters a particle of food and absorbs it automatically. Its mind is minimal if it exists at all. A more elaborate creature like the earthworm can, with patience, be taught to choose its way down a channel, one branch of which leads to discomfort, another to pleasant damp mud. An octopus can learn not to pounce on a piece of fish which is associated with a certain symbol which indicates that to grasp it means an electric shock. Direct, instinctive reflex is here modified by what at a later stage becomes conscious perception. The animal, even in this state, shows a minute power to discriminate between alternatives, and *to judge*. This in turn develops into the deliberate choice between ways, let us say, by which an ape can reach a banana: he may climb up and get it, or he may discover that he can knock it off a shelf with a stick; and he decides which he will do. Eventually we have the kind of mind which is able to think abstractly, placing a mental image of a situation before itself, and then working on this before acting: a mind which is in the literal sense conscious, a subject "knowing with" an object or the image of that object, and looking at it from various angles before acting.

During this process there emerges a factor which is not seen in the first stages: individuality. It is obvious that in the earlier kingdoms, and even a long way up among the animals, the emphasis is on the mass: iron all over the world is the same. Even crystals, the "highest" minerals, varying in size and shape, are built on a stereotyped mold; and in fact, until we reach the vertebrates, basic differences between creatures of the same species are virtually non-existent.

Step by step, individuality emerges, and together with that, the biological group becomes smaller and more differentiated within itself. It seems as if the potentiality of individuality grows slowly out of the depths, at first emerging temporarily like the head of a seal out of the sea, then falling back again. In a flock of birds, starlings for instance, wheeling with almost military precision, one or two may suddenly behave differently from the rest. Among hens there is a clear pecking order. A new cow introduced into a herd may be ostracized for a time, then accepted; or else one of the herd does not do what the rest do. These seem to be signs of incipient individuality. It is more markedly seen in the societies of apes, where there are leaders and sub-leaders, even something like caste, yet where basically, as in human tribal democracy, all are fundamentally equal.

It is only when we come to man, however, that this individuality becomes firmly established and persists even in the most tribalized communities, where custom and convention dominate most of life.

Looking at the matter differently, we say that, in the early stages, incoming impulses produce immediate and automatic reaction of what W. H. Rivers calls a *protopathic* and instinctive nature: all-or-none. A hare may at one moment lie absolutely still. But if danger comes too close, he runs with all his energy in a manner which may be out of proportion to the threat. But step by step there comes a break between incoming stimulus and action. During that break, as we have said, psychic processes take place: past events affect the pattern, *conditioning* the eventual response; perhaps the rudiments of thought and judgment come into play. The result is modified action, varying with external circumstances. It is now becoming *epicritic*, to use Rivers' other term; carefully adapted, so that total muscular strength is not used where less will do what is needed, skill is acquired for difficult tasks. To watch a dog at the bidding of his master holding himself back from the food he wants, is to see epicritic factors at work, and moreover, in conflict as between primitive instinct and a less primitive wish to please his owner. The simple minded animal would merely take the food at once if he wanted it. He would obey the mandate of instinct and not cross its direct expression because of other considerations.

That the primitive or protopathic levels of instinct do not die out is clear when a domestic animal runs amuck and cannot be controlled because it is frightened or aggressive. Even in man the same thing still exists and may break out under stress, especially in certain psychological types. Rivers, to illustrate the thesis that man stands on a thin crust of civilization with, underneath, the instincts of the jungle, tells of an airman, who, by the most skillful and carefully judged maneuvers brought his damaged machine safely to earth. When the danger was over, he leaped out of the plane and ran away from it as fast as he could. His flight was, obviously, absurd except from the standpoint of pure primitive animal fear which, held in check by the epicritic veneer of his mind, broke loose when the tension was relaxed. The animal was there, and not properly absorbed into and integrated with his humanity. It is the same with all of us, even if it does not show: we can lose our heads, be "beside ourselves", we can be carried by herd behavior and do things which afterward appall our civilized, epicritic minds. Our previous individuality becomes swept away by primitive emotions, and we return to a lower evolutionary level. This is a very obvious phenomenon today, not only in undeveloped countries but among educated and sophisticated people. The young are particularly prone to it. It is the cause of uncontrolled mob behavior. Nature has on these occasions been allowed to overwhelm humanity, though fortunately the latter regains control after a while — if we are not to remain insane.

That such a thing can happen suggests that few, if any of us, have yet reached the middle point of our "isthmus." In a magnetic field one of the opposing poles pulls more strongly on an object which is nearer to it than to the center. We are still for the most part nearer the instinctive, primitive pole of life than its opposite. Hence, though we may consciously struggle against the old and regressive pull, it can still win, at least for a time.

At this point we find that a number of different ideas converge. First, there is Teilhard de Chardin's idea that evolution moves from a beginning toward an end. He calls these the alpha and omega states. A continuous thread of life links those ends. We human beings are on that thread, only part of which is yet actualized, the rest being latent. The part already unwound is in the past, leading to the present; the latent part is teleology, the future.

Somewhere along the line, natural development changed its methods. Previously. it secured the process by, so to speak, experimentally bringing about physical changes, developing new organs for flight, aggression, hunting, and many less obvious matters. Many of these experiments led to a dead end: species flourished for a time, then died out. But at each stage there seemed to be a residue which led to a new phase. There came a time however, when it seemed as if, after the primates, physical progress could go no further; organic evolution practically came to a standstill. But the invisible stream of life behind the scenes still pressed forward in one direction, toward cerebral development and the expansion of mind.

We have already seen how thinking begins in the higher animal when he starts to make judgments and choices. There is a correlation between his brain structure and his psychology. Brain tissue, however, seems to change very little after that. When the mind begins to function in a manner much more elaborate than any animal can reach, physical development almost peters out, but mind itself goes on growing, using as its physical basis the already existent computer machine of the nervous system.

The emphasis is now on the mental level rather than on the physical; man sets out on the road toward something beyond mere simple physical survival. He leaves the mythological Garden and becomes human. Erich Fromm puts it neatly, that the first essentially human act was one of disobedience. Man refused to let himself be run by automatic, unthought urges, the commands of God, i.e. Nature, in the kindergarten of Eden. This was due to the fact that he had eaten of the symbolic fruit and for the first time consciously said, "I." The masculine and feminine elements, call them by what name we will, had been separated, became dynamic, and in the field between them I-ness was born.

This individuality became the nucleus of the future mentality. The results are before us today: a mediocre animal, in the bodily sense, has almost taken over the globe and all its denizens. Basically this has happened because mankind turned its attention outward, toward its environment. "Adam delved and Eve span," and their sons became agriculturalists. They learned about natural events and discovered how to adapt them to their own ends, improving on many things, making two blades of wheat grow where one or even none grew before. Physically, instead of growing fresh kinds of fur or greater muscular strength, they used their environment to give them material for clothes and tools.

This expansion outward can be traced through history, with vast acceleration in the last two centuries. The mind nowadays tends to feel out toward infinity; the universe is seen, in the current idiom, as "open-ended," its origin and destiny unknown and perhaps merely thought of because of the finite nature of our mental processes. We have not reached the limits (and probably never will), of the small or the great, the ancient and the future.

Then came the historical shock of two world wars, culminating in the realization of where all this expansion might lead: nowhere, if we go on as we have been going, except into the void.

It is perhaps at this point — taking the point as extending over several decades — that man's thinking starts to turn in another direction, opens up another dimension to explore. He begins to look within himself instead of outward; and here again he learns that the road also leads toward infinity; there is no end in sight, and he is apt to feel, after a time, that his inner being too is open-ended. The problems of life cannot be solved by seeking an end: infinity, in whatever direction we look, is eternally remote. Yet there can be no more than one infinity, a place where all things, the great, the small, the external and the internal meet: a thing inconceivable to the ordinary mind. But, as we shall suggest, there are rare human beings — seers, Rishis, mystics, artists — who seem to have at least an inkling of the solution of the great mystery and try to tell about it.

It is our thesis that such vision can be reached, and must come to be at least a preoccupation, not only for a few, but for mankind collectively. It involves a new form of mentality, the use of new and still largely unsuspected functions of the mind so that we can cross the bridge into a new life, pass beyond the "middle state," and so find the key and the meaning of existence.

Some may say that we are dealing with abstractions which have no reality. The materialist sees only a mechanistic universe, so he says anything else is pure fantasy and supposition. Others, though they cannot prove it to the scientist, know that this is not so. Mechanism there is, but there is something which lies behind mechanism: if there were not, there would be no mechanism. It is in this direction that the following chapters will run, in an endeavor to show how, by practical methods, each man can learn to know this for himself. The means are there — have always been there for the wise to find. Now it is the turn of the rest of us to begin to follow where they lead. We *must,* or we die; we *should,* because it is our task in the vast evolutionary span. But neither God nor man can force us; we must ourselves decide.

Chapter II

THE REALITY OF THE INVISIBLE

It seems, if the thesis presented in the introduction is valid, as if future evolution might for an indefinite period take place behind the scenes of the visible world of material objects. That is, it will proceed in a realm which is invisible to the physical senses. Mind cannot be weighed and measured except in a sketchy and superficial way, as it shows through physical consciousness; hence it is not really susceptible to the methodology of the older forms of science. To some therefore it is felt that it is not *real* in the same way that material objects are real. It is, we are told, subjective, that only material things are objective; and indeed there is some substance to this argument because it is clear that our relation to things of the mind is different from that which we have to the physical world. But this does not dispose of the existence of the subjective world, as an objective reality, which is extremely potent in every aspect of life, including the material. It must therefore be *real* even though it seems to belong to another order of reality than the material.

Fortunately, the truly modern scientist has gone beyond the stage of pure materialism. In many ways he recognizes what others find self-evident, any discussion of which is irrelevant and a waste of time. Some speak frankly about there being a God. They usually do not mean the personal, anthropomorphic god of so many religions. Rather do they postulate a transcendental Intelligence behind the phenomenal world, a Noumenon from which phenomena arise, and from which comes the Natural Law which some prefer to the word *god*. Others may not go so

11

far, but realize that there is, behind the outer forms, a stream of energy without which no creature would be alive.* The difference between a dead body and a live one is that this energy has ceased from ordering and coordinating the matter of which that body is made; so it regresses to a lower level where the same stream operates but without the larger or higher scale ordering of the mass of tissue which is the living body.

It is as evident as it may be startling to some, to realize that the tendency of science today is toward substantiating the attitude of the religionist who speaks in theistic terms, the psychologist to whom mind is a very real and structured organism, the artist who knows that his insights arise from deep within himself, and the psychically sensitive person who perceives the invisible as a world at least partly of matter of a finer grade than the physical, but pervaded also by non-material energies.

The people who deny non-material reality are, in fact a minority among men. They may be intellectually more developed than the primitive savage who dwells unquestioningly in a world populated by invisible spirits, goblins and other entities. They have not, however, reached the degree of intelligence (as against intellect) which lies beyond what they are pleased to call rationalism — and how irrational this is, is usually well known to the rationalist's friends and relations. Even the sophisticated Greeks lived among gods and heroes, nymphs and satyrs, who wove in and out of their lives, unchallenged as to their reality; and this has continued in one or another form right up to the present.

The only key to any kind of understanding of the world is, as we have shown, the human mind. This invisible, intangible, apparently limitless field which is, moreover, the origin of all our thinking is, as we know, an organism as complex in its own way as the physical. Its dependence on an intact brain to express itself in waking consciousness may seem to justify those who equate mind and brain. If the mind can, however, be shown to exist apart from the brain, the whole matter needs to be considered afresh, and there is ample, if only circumstantial, evidence that this can happen. A man with an unconscious body can

---

*See the Reports of the Gifford Lectures, several volumes of which appeared in recent years published by Collins, London.

on occasion retain most if not all the qualities of his mind. He is still himself, he can think and feel and, in some instances, perceive as if through the physical senses, not only the physical environment, but, in a detached way, even his body — and the sense organs of which the necessity is assumed if one is to perceive at all.

One instance, already quoted in the past, was that of the doctor in an air crash, who stepped out of the machine. Seeing people trying to extricate the pilot, he tried to tell them what to do for the best, but failed to make any impression: he was not seen or heard. Then he saw a body on the ground with a man bending over it. Going near, he saw this was himself — including the eyes through which he would normally have seen, though now he was seeing without them — and suddenly found himself back in the body with a mouth full of brandy. His comment, later, was to the effect that he now knew what death was like.

In another case, a sick woman saw, from somewhere near the ceiling of her room, her own body in its bed. She noted that the furniture had been moved around, and that a red rubber tube leading to a mask was being held over her face. Then, in her own words, she "lost consciousness," coming to in the narrow field of awareness of a body with double pneumonia, which was being fed with oxygen.

There is a slight weakness in these cases, as in many others which have been collected by John Vyvyan in *A Case Against Jones*.* This is that they recovered and did not actually die. But there are also a few cases where it is difficult to doubt that communication has been established with a person actually dead in the physical sense, yet very much alive and very much himself in another, non-physical realm.

This is not scientific proof of anything, and especially not of posthumous conditions, but it weighs in the scale with the universal belief — to which Kant said attention should be paid — of the existence of a soul. It makes a reasonable hypothesis at least.

If it is true that human self-identity is the core of the mind, it must follow that the body is not the principal organ of man's

*James Clarke and Co., London.

13

total life. It has become, by an evolutionary process, an aspect only of the totality of himself, subsidiary to the mind and ego, much as the vegetative life is to the animal organism. It belongs to past rather than future evolution, even though it remains the all-important link between the mind and the physical world. The body has been built up out of the demands of instinct, and relies on the instinctive mind. But mind itself is now reaching beyond the level of instinct, which should occupy a secondary place in future evolution. Yet in its instinct-based form it remains a great and dynamic force which serves us well in daily life. The human problem today is that we still incline to allow instinct to be our master instead of our servant. How it operates we shall now consider.

Chapter III

INSTINCTIVE MAN

It will be well therefore if, before proceeding further, we try to obtain a clear picture both of the part instinct plays in man, and of the part played by man in adapting instinct to his own ends.

Animal instinct is a basic urge to survive physically. It can be divided under various subheadings such as sex, aggression, hunger, the instinct to fly from danger or to hunt for food; but these are only different channels toward the basic end, which is to preserve, if not the single animal, then the group or species. One might add a special form of instinct, which is to adapt to environment, out of which new species and varieties arise.

Now man, already described as a mediocre animal, enters the scene. As we have already said, he differs from the animal in having in himself the focus we call the ego, the sense of *I-ness* as a separate being, already foreshadowed in the higher animals but becoming increasingly important only in humanity. More than this, yet doubtless connected with the ego, man is the first creature to have a thirst for knowledge for its own sake. Many animals are to some degree inquisitive, they discover how to do things in new ways. Man alone, however, shows the characteristic which eventually makes him a pure scientist, regardless of how that science can be applied. Essentially, this means that there is that in man which urges him on into expanding fields. These he covers with his mind first, with his body perhaps thereafter. He embarks on exploration for no other reason than that there is something to be explored. In other words, he wants ever to expand his conscious field, to change its character, to refine and to add constantly to it. All the tools and the detecting instruments he creates are, in effect, extensions of himself, his mind projected into the external material world and embracing a field wider than his own body allows.

These factors are, clearly, something different from, and new to the animal pattern of life; yet, not only at first but still today they rest largely on this pattern, weaving its strands into new designs and relationships.

These new forms arise out of the action of mind in humanized form. The ego serves as a fulcrum lacking in the animal. It is the point from which mental activity radiates, as well as that on which it focuses.

Primitive man shows little of this power of self. The individual spends his life within the confines of tribal dictates and customs, only beginning to break out as the ego becomes stronger and more assertive. As this happens, he finds himself more or less of an outsider in his community, which may lead to his being disowned by it or, on the other hand, may raise him into the position of a leader and reformer. Professor J. E. Marcault, in a privately circulated paper, argues that what in contemporary idiom is often called the "lunatic fringe" of society consists of nonconformists to tribal law, whether in the African bush, the South American jungles, the City of London or the universities. Some keep their touch with the group and so are the vanguard of progress, some lose it and are the unbalanced, anti-social element which includes the neurotics, psychotics and delinquents in our midst. In all cases, this vanguard is due to the assertion of individuality moving out of the rut of mass, instinctive life, sometimes in a positive, sometimes in a negative direction. Stuart Holroyd, in his first book, *Emergence from Chaos,* argues this matter in a very pointed way.

Returning now to the basic evolutionary purpose of instinct, let us consider human institutions up to the point they have now reached. The first act of self-assertion occurred in terms of the myth of the Garden of Eden. Adam, under the guidance of his feminine intuition, stirred into action by the Serpent — always a symbol of wisdom, not of evil — took, with Eve, a step toward true humanity. Both, knowing themselves, having said "I" for the first time, found themselves in some ways cut off from their natural roots and thrust out into the world. But they realized that they were now in a position to act upon this world out of their own experience. In this way our symbolic ancestors started to make their survival more likely, not by developing bodily prowess, but by using their minds.

It is not difficult from this point to trace out the development of civilization by stages which are still to be found on earth today. First we have entirely nomadic tribes; then those which settle for a time and cultivate the land until it is exhausted before moving on; then more permanent settlements arise, where the land is taken care of and its nutriment replenished when needed. Then we can see how, as intelligence grows, it seems sensible for the strong man to hunt or become a warrior, others, less strong, to take on building, weaving, to be providers of food, and the like. So civilization begins: life in a *civis* where services are exchanged and everybody does not have to do everything for himself and his own family. Barter or exchange is the means of operation in primitive communal life.

Following this, a curious phenomenon occurs: the invention of money. It is curious because it shows that abstract thought begins to impinge on simple physical life. Among many primitive groups, very common and valueless objects like cowrie shells are used as currency, acceptable because of a mental convention between people. Later, gold becomes the symbol of money. This is a metal relatively rare, highly decorative, yet quite useless for making a ploughshare, or a sword or any article of common use. And today, even gold has largely vanished except as a remote token of credit, a word derived from *credo,* the mental act of belief. (It is a puzzle to the non-economist to realize that millions of dollars or pounds appear and disappear in a few hours on the stock exchange, until one sees that money is a *fiction,* a creation of the mind of man, not a material commodity: literally a fiction — from *facio,* "I make" — and only real in an abstract and symbolic sense.)

While this goes on and regulates certain aspects of physical life, man evolves institutions, laws, even abstract creeds and philosophies. He develops industries out of his growing knowledge of the physical world, and these make existence easier, safer,

17

and pleasanter. In other words, his life is largely focused on the basic instinct of self-preservation and self-perpetuation. This base is transformed almost beyond recognition, yet it remains the root of everything he holds dear except for one thing, to which we shall give attention in the next chapter.

In two things, however, man differs from the subhuman kingdoms: his search for security centers around his sense of self, not his body only, and is often only indirectly connected with the body; the other is that, over many millennia he has, in his search for security, elaborated a mind of vast dimensions and power which, moreover, does not seem to be within sight of any final state.

This is instinctive man, a force in the evolutionary process, a creator of things which Nature alone could not create, a destroyer too, on a greater scale than Nature. In any case, he seems to stand for the great originator in what we may look upon as a secondary creation taking place within the field of the greater, cosmic creation, the universe. Without him something would be lost in the evolutionary process; this fact justifies what a deep-thinking if unorthodox Christian priest once said, that man is as necessary to God as God is to man.

Chapter IV

ESSENTIAL MAN

In the last chapter we said that all that man holds most dear can, with one exception, be comprehended within the sphere of instinct. This exception is a certain order of experience which does not fit in with basic instinctive patterns however much transformed. It cannot be remotely connected with self-preservation; it may, on the contrary, be felt as a challenge to the ego and the values it has accumulated round itself. Yet those who experience and accept it feel that it is the most precious and vital thing which has happened to them. It is, in terms of ordinary life, quite useless. What, for instance, is the value of aesthetic appreciation, of a sense of the poetic, the artistic, the religious, compared with such things as money, power, prestige, material freedom and so on? To the materialist, there is none. The one who has the experience, however, would say that it is worth more than anything in the ordinary world, however pleasurable and desirable.

We refer to the kind of event which Abraham Maslow has called "peak experience," giving it a name which has the virtue of not being specific, and so covering many aspects of what amounts to the same thing. It occurs to artists, mystics, lovers, to people in moments of great happiness or, equally, to others in great suffering. There is the same quality in these inner events, in that they reveal that behind the workaday, discursive stream of experience there is another and more deeply meaningful world. We become conscious of it at times, and find ourselves functioning at a mental level which is quite different from that of our usual habit. It gives a sense of greater reality than the normal, reducing the latter to the level of what Aldous Huxley describes as "cheap plastic." Even logic falls away, though the new vision is anything but irrational; it transcends logic and leaves it where it belongs, a useful thing for daily life, here replaced by something far more potent and valuable.

The vision is in itself beyond direct expression; yet, when the glimpse — for it is rarely more — is over, and we return to our usual level of awareness, something of it may be told in the language of ordinary life. The mystics sometimes make exclamatory remarks such as we find in Aldous Huxley's *The Perennial Philosophy* and Raynor Johnson's *Watcher on the Hills* — books which correlate what many have said, and show the similarity of quality in all their experiences. For the peak moment lifts one out of the personal field, without either destroying or disregarding it, into a state where the keynote is universality and hence is to be shared with every other human being.

Coming now closer to the individual, the peak experience is something which is reached unexpectedly, "in a moment, in the twinkling of an eye." It is called by many names: "The Vision," Tao, Satori, Illumination, Moksha, Buddhi, Union with God, the Existential Moment, and so on. The name does not matter, but the event stands out like the isolated peaks one sees when flying up the west coast to America: snow-covered and majestic, towering over the ranges of the Sierra lying blue and brown at their feet.

Unexpectedness is one of its features. It is important to understand this, as one cannot, through any mental exercise or devotion evoke it at will. Indeed, expectancy, let alone any sense one has a right to it, must almost inevitably frustrate. "The wind bloweth where it listeth and thou hearest the voice thereof, but knowest not whence it cometh and whither it goeth." The wind, or *pneuma,* a word which also means Spirit, obeys its own laws, and we do not know these laws — as yet — if for no better reason than that we have so far concentrated our attention on the material, the bodily, and the demands of instinctive nature.

It is only the rare individual who knows the rules of this timeless world. But even he, if he is overwhelmed by his Vision, finds himself hampered. He may become so absorbed by it that he loses touch with the everyday world and with commonsense.

This means that because of what he sees, he is not, in the electrical sense, "earthed." His physical existence therefore lacks the dynamism that he might bring into it; for unless in some way physical life is changed by the Vision, the latter is not complete. It may in fact then become more a detriment than anything else, until the individual discovers that what is truly spiritual includes all aspects of ordinary life and allows none to become lost even while it transforms him.

This brings us to a consideration of the space-time aspect of peak experiences. There are some instances where it takes place in a minute fraction of time. Warner Allen* tells us that his experience occurred "between two demi-semi-quavers" while listening to a Beethoven symphony in the Queen's Hall, London. Rupert Brooke, in *Dining-Room Tea* says something similar; the fire, the falling stream of tea between pot and cup, the movement of people, all froze for an instant while he *saw*. On the other hand, it can happen that somebody may remain in a state of exalted consciousness for an hour or more without realizing that time has passed. Time thus seems to fade into eternity, spreading backward and forward from the *now* without ever reaching beginning or end.

In the same way space may resolve itself into a mathematical, dimensionless point, which is *here,* wherever we are; or it may, alternatively, be felt to expand so that *here* spreads infinitely through the extended universe. The result is the same, that *I* and the worlds are at the same time infinitely great, and also resolved into the minute dot which is *myself*.

These things mean that, in some state of consciousness, we feel that we are omniscient, we are God, infinite, eternal. There is no other God than my-Self, or conversely, I am completely at-one with God. At the same time, the totality of this God-Self is in every creature equally, not merely a part of It, but wholly. Mystics who have had the temerity to try to say these things have, in the past at least, paid heavy penalties for what others have felt to be blasphemy rather than profound truth. This is a very practical reason for bringing the sense of the Vision into the realm of ordinary life, showing its effect by a change in the way one behaves and not leaving it out of reach in some higher

The Timeless Moment, Faber & Faber, London.

sphere: it may be misunderstood if it is merely talked about.

A third, surprising aspect of the matter is that, though the Vision is quite new, it is also utterly familiar; and, though it contains all the complexities of life, it is also extremely simple, and so obvious that one wonders how one can ever not have been aware of it.

Then it can be felt as an experience with deeply religious content. One may, as some do, refer to it as "seeing God," yet one is not confronted with any personal Deity, let alone the kind fashioned out of the ordinary mind of man and worshipped in most temples and churches.

Lastly, what of the beholder? In a paradoxical way, he is all the time himself, a being with identity. But this identity is quite different from the *I* of ordinary daily affairs. The personal ego exists separate from and contrasted with other egos, and apart from a world which is external to it. This new Self is completely at one with its environment. In some indescribable way it is, as we have said, at once itself and everything in the universe. But it is still self-identity, the psychological ego exalted to a higher octave, and so transfigured.

Beside this — and it might be taken as the test of validity of the inner experience — the one who has really apprehended the Vision cannot feel pride or superiority. He knows he is at one with the highest transcendental Power, but he must at the same time genuinely feel that he is the equal of the most humble worm at his feet, not by lip service only, but deeply so, throughout himself. If he does not, he is in serious danger. *Hubris* is probably the "sin against the Holy Ghost," which, we are told, can never be forgiven; for, until it is resolved and eliminated, it stands forever between us and the fullness of Truth. On the contrary, the true seer will recognize what is meant when, as one writer puts it, he learns to know God not *in* but *as* stone, or water, or a tree or any other creature.

To sum up, peak experience represents an order of consciousness and Self-identity which is different from that of the humdrum levels of earth-based, instinctive life. At these moments we are still ourselves, but our whole perception is different in a new-old way, complexity resolves into a simplicity which still has room for complexity. Our minds are still minds, since the main features of mental activity are there, but they function in a manner indescribable except by paradox, one of which is that it is deeply *felt* yet there is no *emotion* about it. It is still, poised, yet not inert, and not connected with the "moving out" which is the root of the word *emotion*. It is all *here* and *now,* where one IS.

Were we able to live permanently in this illuminated state, we might label ourselves Essential Man, though to do this now would, except for the very few, be as premature as it is for our species to flatter itself that it is *homo sapiens*, "*wise* man."

Though it may seem from what we have said that this whole matter is exceptional, vastly revolutionary, and outside the reach of ordinary people, it is not so. We have, for purposes of clarity, tried to paint a large scale picture of this other state of consciousness, but something of it reaches us fairly often in daily life, unrecognized perhaps as other than an event which touches us deeply. There are peaks at all levels, whether the summit be Snowdon, the Matterhorn or Mount Everest. What matters is the quality of "peakness," something which stays with us and in some measure changes our inner and outer life. As intelligence and sensitivity grow, we can learn to discriminate between this kind of event, however small, and the emotional splurge which some people enjoy and believe to be both spiritually enlightening and necessary to artistic creation. Emotion is not necessary to true creativity, it can be merely a meretricious substitute for what is real, deep, and above all, still, yet deeply felt, with "thoughts that do often lie too deep for tears."

Chapter V

BEING AND EXISTENCE

These two words, hackneyed and much in use today, still have a value when applied to the two levels of experience of which we have written. To use them, however, does not mean that the writers are existentialists in the sense of adhering to a wordy philosophy difficult to understand and to disentangle from other viewpoints. An "ism" is a cult, and life cannot be enclosed in any cult. The words can, however, be linked with principles adumbrated in older and more traditional philosophies.

Being can be defined as the state realized during peak experience. It is still, as the center of a revolving wheel is still; unitary or single; outside space-time as we ordinarily know it, but not of necessity outside some other order of it which lies beyond our ken; hence, Being is not subject to division or to the mutabilities of time; and so, to use the ordinary words, it stands for both universality and immortality.

Consciousness of Being seems to us from our present usual frame of mind unlimited, illumined, a state where there is no end to what we comprehend and know. It is blissful — the best word to set against mere pleasure or pain. It is the realm of Spirit as distinct from that of soul or mind (these terms being equivalent) which, with the body, make the personality. It gives the sense of having confronted the Numinous or Divine, so marked in many of the accounts we have been given.

Further, it is outside the field of causality and the level where effect follows cause; yet it can be called the Prime Cause of everything else, Leonardo da Vinci's *Primo Motore,* whence all causes and effects arise.

In another terminology we can speak of Being as the place of Essence: a word derived from the Latin *esse,* to be. The *Oxford Dictionary* defines Essence as "absolute Being," "reality underlying phenomena," "all that makes a thing what it is," "intrinsic nature" — philosophical terms which become highly meaningful and practical to the one who has had real vision.

Existence, on the other hand, is where our minds ordinarily function. The word, derived from Latin *ex*, out and *sto*, I stand, seems to reflect an intuitive sense that to exist is to be on the outside of something else, that something being Essence or Being. It is a place where, naturally, cause produces effect which, in turn may be the cause which produces further effect, in an endless chain, each link in which is part of a Wholeness which is Being, God, the Prime Cause.

It follows that existence can be expressed in terms of division between two poles, cause and effect being such a pair. This is the basis of the Taoist philosophy in its simplest form. Essential Tao is here conceived as manifesting, through its quality of Teh, in a polarity called *yang* and *yin,* masculine and feminine, positive and negative, according to the role played in any phenomenon such as subject and object, I and not-I. The unenlightened person lives in this polarized, phenomenal world, his whole existence weaving back and forth between pairs of opposites. When enlightenment is reached — as, momentarily it is glimpsed by many — the Tao behind these opposites is known, and essential Reality is found.

In India, this polarized world is called *maya,* often translated "illusion," which is correct, but an over-simplification of the concept. It is illusion in the sense that it means incomplete understanding and vision, less-than-absolute reality, or, better for our purposes, polarized reality. *Yin-yang* is *maya,* the existential plane, the place where we human beings live as instinctive men and women in the sense we have used that phrase.

We can thus see a world where there are an infinite number of phenomena, cause-and-effect pairs, the *cause* being active, *yang*; the *effect* receptive, feminine, *yin.* But as an effect becomes the cause of further results, the *yin* becomes *yang,* the new effect being *yin.* Ultimately, the polarity resolves into the Tao which stands, as it were, at the apex of a triangle at the base of which *yin* and *yang* shuttle to and fro from one end to the other. We are reminded here of the Buddhist wheel of rebirth — that is, of existence — from which there is no escape except when one enters Nirvana, Pure Being.

Tao has been described as the "reconciling principle" behind *yin-yang* phenomenalism. This suggests a compromise between contending forces, but Tao means far more than that. It is better seen as That which contains, supports and maintains the pairs for as long as they are operative. In Tao, the opposites do not cancel out into colorless negation, the "good" against the "evil," the pleasant against the painful. They are integrated into a higher synthesis, translated into a higher dimension, where both have their rightful place and balance: this is what we call Tao, Being or Essence. It is also the Numen, God.

There are thus an infinite number of points at which Tao or God can be discovered by the inwardly open eye. But this eye is not the same as the eye which sees and, indeed, learns, through the polarities of existence. It is related to it as the personal ego is to the essential Self, but like true Self, it operates in other dimensions.

Ordinary sight (using this sense for our discussion, as convenient, and also as representing the central place of all perception, the ordinary mind) depends on polarity or differentiation even where Essential matters are concerned. In a well-known experiment, a beam of light is shone through a vacuum jar. It is visible before it reaches the jar, vanishes inside it and reappears as it emerges through the glass on the far side. If, then, some dust or steam is let into the vacuum, the beam at once shows up. This is because the "pure" light is interfered with. The particles not only reflect and refract the light, they produce places of non-light or shadow, so that the beam becomes "manifest" and visible. Tao has polarized into *yin-yang,* and we perceive. The light shows us what we call shadow, the shadow shows us light, a reciprocal effect, and one basic to all existential life.

The workaday mind learns to perceive only through contrast, polarity, the division of things into opposites. Without this, things may Be, but we remain unconscious of them. Yet we do not really *understand* until we lift our minds and the concept of these opposites into a new dimension. This is still today a rare event. It is as if we became able to know our beam of light in its pristine form, undisturbed and hence shadowless: a thing no ordinary thinking or physical means can achieve. Yet such understanding can be reached by a form of alchemy — the real, philosophical Alchemy, not that concerned with metallic ores — which moves the mind, not on the horizontal axis between the poles, but vertically, between existence and Being.

The first need is to realize that there are these two levels and modes of mental operation; the second is to discover and use the means, which exist, of making a bridge between the two. It is necessary, also, to remind ourselves that the concept of the division between Being or Essence and existence is itself an example of the polarity required by language, which belongs to the existential level. From the essential angle, both Essence and existence merge into a synthesis and are seen together as aspects of a unitary field of awareness.

Chapter VI

BOTH SIDES OF CONSCIOUSNESS

In our ordinary thinking, we equate the idea of consciousness with being aware in the physical world through an intact brain. This is not really adequate since, as we have pointed out, it seems to be fairly certain that one is able to be conscious apart from the brain, hence that consciousness is primarily in the *mind* and not in the body. The body is the mechanism through which mental consciousness penetrates into the physical world as far as the brain permits, and no further. The body is not conscious any more than a car, however responsive to its driver, is conscious.

The things of which we are aware in normal waking life are, we have every reason to believe, only a fraction of what the mind contains. Behind this relatively small field there lies, as most — but, surprisingly, not all — psychiatrists believe, the unconscious mind, far from "unconscious" if by that is meant absence of awareness within its own field. What is in it contains a great deal of material which does not emerge directly but only in a roundabout way through the brain. The unconscious is considered by some as a limbo of things forgotten by being dropped out of sight as attention focuses elsewhere — such things as a friend's telephone number which can usually not be recalled by frontal attack, but springs out when one is thinking of something else. But beside this, there is a mass of thoughts and feelings which would upset the personal ego of the individual, and which he is unwilling or unable to face directly and recognize as part of himself. This is achieved by active repression or suppression and is something much more powerful than mere passive forgetting.

The psychiatric concept of the unconscious is supported from a different angle by those who report experiences such as we have already outlined, during illness or injury, as also under drugs, hypnosis or in mediumistic trance. To them direct mental or psychic awareness free from the brain is much wider and more extensive than the little which is experienced in waking life.

We are thus presented with a picture of consciousness comparable with what can be seen through the window of a house: a field limited by a certain framework. Looking in, one sees only part of the whole room; looking out, only a piece of the landscape. Moreover, using the same analogy, much will depend also on the clarity of the panes; that is, on the responsiveness of the brain mechanism. Dull senses let in only blurred pictures of the world outside — the physical — while a fuddled brain only lets out a foggy idea of inner mental processes, or uncoordinated attempts to act.

There is more than that. The glass is not an inert, passive film between two worlds. It behaves like a living organism, a tissue, if we like, similar to the physical skin or the membrane round a cell. It has the power to some extent to select certain categories of percepts or ideas and to allow them comparatively free passage, while blocking others. It becomes relatively opaque while attention is focused on the physical world during waking life, more translucent when, during sleep, the senses are in abeyance. Drugs, toxins, foods affect it. So do mental acts like meditation, hypnotic dissociation, mediumistic practices and those which induce a form of hysteria as in some systems in vogue today.

In short, it seems as if there were, between physical waking consciousness and the mind itself an active, living diaphragm, a kind of internal skin, which separates the two. The ego seems able to function on either or both sides of it, standing like the Roman god Janus at the gate of the city, with one face turned inward, the other out into the countryside. It guards the gate with more or less success by day, with less efficacy at night, when dreams filter past and are remembered on waking. These occur during a stage recorded by the electro-encephalogram between deep, dreamless sleep and full waking awareness.

Freud was the first modern scientist to draw scientific attention to these incursions from beyond the veil which we call dreams, and to argue that, however seemingly absurd, every dream indicates in cryptic form something of what is going on in the unconscious mind. In doing this, he was, of course, only confirming an old and popular belief. (Scientists have a way of doing this and, using new terms, feel they have made a new discovery about something, whereas it is in reality already well known. But in doing so, they often add a rational explanation to something accepted previously on faith but not carefully thought out.) In the case of dreams, we have the statement of a problem, a point of stress within the mind; and, like all problems, dreams contain the key to it. Nightmares may be said to be dreams without a key, which is why one seems unable to escape from the situation shown. In that sense, a dream may be looked on as a symptom of what, if serious, we label neurosis or lack of integration. This does not mean that every dreamer is therefore clinically a neurotic: but who is there who is entirely free from inner conflict? The "normal" person only exists in theory and we all deviate from him to a greater or less degree. It may be surmised that a fully realized human being would therefore either not dream at all or else be aware of his inner mental processes all through waking life, leaving no censorship to be circumvented at night. Hence any dream would represent directly a psychic experience and would not be "veiled in allegory and illustrated by symbol," as now: it would not be a dream but a direct form of perception.

It seems evident, when the matter is studied in this way, that the ego, the personal representative of the essential Self, is one of the factors affecting the diaphragm between the conscious and the unconscious mind. It tries to keep before us a pleasant picture of ourselves, to build up a mask-self or *persona* with which to meet the world and the people outside ourselves. It is limited, however, by forces it cannot control: damage to the brain or sense organs, which let too much or too little pass through; emotional pressures from within, which cause symptoms of neurosis; and so on. Complete breakdown may occur as a result of such things as chemical poisoning — including that by psychedelic drugs — toxins such as those of syphilis; or from inside the mind by too great a conflict of emotions, with the result that psychosis occurs. "Invasion from the unconscious," is Jung's definition of psychosis. Some methods of yoga meditation, deep breathing of the wrong sort, or the "processing" of scientology as well as the "opening" in subud, are all equally wrong and dangerous.

In any case, there is a functional division between objective or waking consciousness, and subjectivity. The subjective is also consciousness, but of a different quality, being more plastic and fluidic than is that of the physical world, where things are not so clearly divided into what is I and what is not-I.

The physical world is, to our minds, "real." It contains *rera* (singular, *res,* a thing) which are constant, stable, self-existent, and which we feel are definitely outside what we call ourselves. We perceive them through the senses, we act upon them and they react on us. But they are not, except in this way, within our personal orbit. If we are philosophically inclined, we shall carry our thought further and add that what we know of these objects is by means of an image largely created in the subjective mind on the basis of sense data. These data are in themselves valid but scrappy and incomplete. We do not see things as they really are, as witnessed by our idea of solid matter which, we now know, is in fact mainly space empty of everything except energy-waves. The sense data themselves, as they make their impact on the brain, are only the first step in creating our eventual image and presenting it to what we call "I," the ego.* After this the ego as it were returns its percepts to the screen of the physical world, on which an image can be focused and made clear.

This subjective view may seem to be contradicted by the fact that damage to certain parts of the brain, notably the temporal lobe, brings back into physical consciousness memories which are relived as if distance in time were abolished. One is not looking back into the past but bringing the past up into the

*A simple experiment can be performed which shows the role of the mind in physical perception. If we look at a piece of floor or a tabletop or fabric in which the pattern suggests hexagonal tiles, it is easy to "see" this pattern in terms of a central hexagon surrounded by "petals" identical in shape and color and size — other tiles. By a mental act, the central unit can then be displaced so that it becomes the petal of another set of seven tiles, making a similar "flower." Then, again by mental action, the pattern can be made to consist of rows of tiles running across, down, or diagonally across the surface.

Clearly, the sense percepts have in no way changed during our exercise. But by using our minds, we have altered the form in which we assess and arrange them. If emotional factors enter the process, we can readily understand how facts become distorted, however well they might be authenticated, say by a photographic record of an event.

present. This suggests that the brain itself stores memory in the same mechanical way, as does a computer. But computers are not intelligent or conscious. What takes place here has the same quality that we find in dreams, time being telescoped as if it were flexible and plastic and, as it were, alive. It would be unwise to be dogmatic, but putting all considerations together, they suggest that such phenomena as are caused by brain injury are at least as likely to be due to thinning of the veil between waking consciousness and the subjective world as to some mysterious storage faculty of the brain cells themselves.

This is how things appear, viewed from outside, and from the sphere of physical awareness. But subjective experience has its own validity, and if we try now to look at things from within the psyche — the wider field which includes, but extends beyond, physical consciousness — it seems to work as if there were a floor between itself and the physical world. It can function in some measure through that floor by means of the brain, but access is not altogether free. This coincides with our sense that things in the material world are outside ourselves, and hence real in their own right.

It becomes very evident that the inner, subjective realm of the mind is of a very different nature from the field of physical consciousness. For, normally, people are unaware of there being anything in it outside themselves. The mind apparently *is* that world and the objects in it are created by it. To *me* there are *my* images, *my* thoughts, *my* feelings, even if they should derive originally from a physical percept. It is only if I have considerably more insight that I may become aware of the fact that this personal mental field consists of things I have feelings about, and which cluster around my ego, but that there are other minds, other similar clusters which are the personal minds of others. There is no sharp division between myself and them such as I find exists at the physical level. I learn both by experience and if I study psychology, about group and herd phenomena, that each individual mind seems to be at this level an entity which holds together by something akin to gravity, drawing certain things which I call "mine," about my personal ego. There is no containing "skin" around my mind, but, like a planetary system, it centers around a sun which draws the planets around it. The ego is that sun. Between these personalities there is, seemingly, a sea of what is called today "collective mind" in which I and others float like clumps of seaweed in the ocean, without a clear-cut edge between us. Further, what others put out into this ocean influences me; and I, in turn, influence them. Should I become aware of this transference of thought and feeling in my waking brain, I call it telepathy. When, as usual, I am not so aware, it still operates, but I would then call it mass emotion or thought, being with people — or against them — as they react to fashions and trends, or as a mob. Whether I know it or not, I am carried by such currents — until I have achieved sufficient mental objectivity to be largely self-contained, and so, self-directing.

Such seems to be the main difference between what we normally call consciousness — meaning by that the fragment of the whole which penetrates to the waking brain — and the highly active and conscious "unconscious" mind. The "membrane" between the two is very important to mental and physical health and balance. It would never do to have the carefully filtered material which reaches consciousness upset by a wholesale riot of the inner mind. We need, for evolutionary purposes, to keep the two at least in some measure apart in a way which is probably unnecessary to the pre-egoic animal. Only so can evolution proceed. This, for mankind, means that only so can the mind develop around the center of individuality which we know first as the ego. This, in turn, requires a separation of self from the mass, that is, objectivity. The value of the physical world, and of our peculiar relation to it acts as a starting point for this, enabling us to become "scientific" before we carry this same mental power, to be able to observe with detachment, into other and less clear-cut fields. Hence the need of the ego, as the growing-point of the individual, to try to draw a veil between the inner and outer and to achieve clear-cut objective awareness where we can, i.e. between brain consciousness of the physical world, and the inner mind.

Things seem to happen in the waking field which we cannot — yet, at any rate — achieve elsewhere. If we consider how we learn and acquire new skills, i.e. become more and more human, we find that the first requisite is to pay careful attention to what is wanted and learn how to perform certain acts. We can only do this while we are fully awake. We could never learn to ride a bicycle or how to add up a column of figures during sleep; though it is true that we seem to be able, while we are asleep, to work on information we have collected, and so perhaps wake up understanding it better. The maxim to "sleep on it," where a problem is concerned, is sound advice. Essentially, we have to learn by diligent conscious application. Then gradually, as our brains become trained, we can relax and allow matters to become increasingly automatic. When one has really mastered a job, one can do most or all of it without conscious attention. The mind and brain are now "conditioned," and a part of the unconscious which is really *sub*conscious can take over. Thus we can then drive a car safely on a busy road while discussing abstract philosophical matters. Indeed, one cannot be a good driver — or typist, or anything else — until the actions become automatic and do not need to be thought out in detail at every step.

This suggests that, starting at a low evolutionary level of simple reflex actions such as we see in primitive animals, we build up a hierarchy of increasingly complex integrated chains of association and response, with waking consciousness as it were floating on top of them. As new things are learned, we allow them to fall, silting down, as it were, into the true *sub*conscious levels of the mind. That this is so seems confirmed in reverse by the fact that even such deeply vegetative functions as breathing, the heart beat, and digestive processes, can be brought up from the depths and once more be controlled by the conscious mind. This is seen in the phenomena produced by fakirs and sadhus and other practitioners of low forms of yoga —though of what use this is except to *épater le bourgeois* and extract money from him it is difficult to see.

So we can define the *sub*conscious mind as that part of the totality which contains instinct, past experience, memory, training. But man also has many powers still latent. They have never yet become explicit and so entered waking consciousness. They represent the future, and lie in that part of the mind we look upon as Essential. This we may well call the *super*conscious which, with the subconscious and the "forgettery" make up the total field of the *un*conscious mind.

There is a point worth studying where the superconsciousness is concerned. For just as there appears to be a "floor" to the field in which the ordinary mind normally operates, so there seems to be a ceiling between itself and the other level which we have called the *Essential*. The reason for suggesting this, is that we are not usually aware of its existence except at the rare moments when we transcend the usual patterns of thought and feeling. There is an obstacle between the two levels which seems to correspond to that between the subjective mental world and the dense physical. It occasionally opens up and we experience superconsciousness directly, but usually, even though we are not conscious of the fact, we are probably influenced by it the whole time.

Indeed, in our waking state, we are constantly affected by factors from all levels of the unconscious mind. They operate as an attempt to balance the occurrences in the conscious field, a kind of "anti-consciousness" perhaps comparable to the "anti-matter" which is the present concern of physicists. Psychoanalysts look upon these unconscious processes as arising from past events; but teleology, the future, also plays a part which increases its manifestations as the mind develops. What we have named Essential consciousness thus constantly plays into the existential field and merges with it. Eventually when these factors attain a certain intensity, the whole balance of the unconscious mind swings over toward what to us now appears to be the Essential or spiritual. The overall pattern then changes, the old mind being transformed permanently toward the state we now only perceive intermittently and at special moments. One aspect of this experience which gradually extends shows us that waking life is in reality a kind of sleep, wrapped up in limitations.

We may thus divide consciousness into three zones. These are, in a sense, geographical and theoretical like the division between temperate and tropical zones, rather than hard and fast lines. We have spoken as if there were a "membrane" between them, but we must remember that this is semi-permeable, to use the technical term; it is not like a brick wall. There is constant interchange between each zone, the degree of this depending on the state of the dividing factor, which is at some times more permeable than at others. It seems, too that the "floor" and "ceiling" of the inner psyche are inter-related, so that when a person is most sensitively aware of the Numinous and Essential, he is equally so to physical conditions, and vice versa. Of the three zones, the widest is that of Essence: in fact, as far as we can estimate it, it has no boundaries. The intermediate, psychic realm, between floor and ceiling is more restricted, conditioned by a number of factors derived from what has been called psychological heredity, which means racial background and intrinsic memory extending nobody knows how far back, and also by personal reactions to family and other environment. Clearly, too, physical, somatic influences play into the mind: illness, handicaps, and all the things affecting the ability of the inner self to touch the physical world in which the body lives. And there are also the indefinable "clouds of glory" to which Wordsworth refers as "trailing" behind the newborn child. They seem to reflect something deep and central, not traceable to anything else but the pattern of his own individuality, a reflection of his Essence or true Self. Finally, we have the narrowest field of all, that we know as waking consciousness or, commonly, as consciousness without any adjective. This has the virtue of clarity and of clear focus, and is the fulcrum on which our minds become operative and strong.

The sense of selfhood seems able in principle, if not so freely in practice, to be able to slide up and down on a thread linking these zones. It is sometimes, at one extreme, the personal ego, which carries out physical functions of all kinds; a slightly less well defined self in the intermediate state of sleep or abstraction in thought or feeling; and at the other extreme it is the Self or spiritual Ego, dwelling at the level of Being itself. "I," as a human being, am intrinsically capable of moving from one level to the other; but I have to learn how to overcome the obstacles, or better, to remove them, where they lie between the different zones. This I do with the power which resides in my mind.

Chapter VII.

JACOB'S LADDER

Jacob "dreamed, and behold, a ladder set up on earth, and the top of it reached to heaven; and behold, the angels of God ascending and descending on it. And behold, the Lord stood above it, and said, 'I am the Lord, the God of Abraham . . . And behold, I am with thee, and will keep thee withersoever thou goest, and will bring thee again into this land, for I will not leave thee until I have done that which I have spoken to thee of . . . ' "

(Gen. 28.23)

In the last chapter we have suggested that man, as a total entity, lives in at least three worlds: the physical, the psychic, the spiritual; and that between the three there seems to be, perhaps not a wall, but an area of difficulty to the sense of selfhood and of consciousness as it moves up and down between them. The barrier between the physical and the psychic or mental realm we have already examined, seeing how it can be made opaque, translucent if not transparent, and even breached. That between the psychic and the spiritual is of a different quality. It is also more difficult to study since, while physical evolution and experience belong to the past of the race, spiritual development and realization are things which, it seems, we have to achieve in the future. We only pierce the division at peak moments, whereas we straddle the psycho-physical levels constantly and in all kinds of ways, both natural and artificial. But as we have also suggested, there are means by which personal, psychic, existential life can become consciously linked with Essential, spiritual Being.

These means can be summed up under the one word Religion. The capital is important, in that, while religions of all kinds

37

are, at least supposedly, concerned with Religion, they only too often become lost, as Paul Tillich tells us, in creeds, formulae, rituals which, however profound and clear they may be, stand in the way of pristine, pure religious or spiritual experience, that is, of peak experience.

The word *religion* is, etymologically, derived from *re*, "once more," or "again," and *ligare* "to bind." Otherwise, it means "to re-unite," and clearly implies that it brings together things which, once united, have parted company. If they have not already been together, they could not be *re*-united. The myth of the Prodigal comes to mind: the son becoming estranged from his home, eventually returning and being once more merged into it. This can be understood in terms of the difference between Being or Essence and existence: the basic and unawakened "I" projects itself, or is projected by evolutionary forces, from the inner realm of Being into that of existence, with all its problems of polarity and duality. This is in order to develop individuality and self-consciousness, which it would not acquire by remaining quiescent at "Home."

Religion is not a matter of belief expressed as a creed, or observances, still less of an authoritarian system where the individual is expected to do what he is told, and the priesthood promises to see to it that he enters paradise at death. It is more an attitude of mind, a search for Truth resulting from turning away from purely material and selfish pursuits. This can take any form. There is an Indian saying that "There are as many paths to God as there are lives of the children of men," which rings truer than the claim of Christians or Moslems that theirs is the only way. Indeed, Gandhi is said to have answered a questioner that, yes, he was a Christian, but also a Hindu, a Moslem, a Buddhist, a Jew, a Parsi, and all the rest. Another Indian, a dancer and an artist, said that he saw the way to his own *moksha* or liberation into heaven simply in following the path of his art as a dancer, not through temple worship or private meditation. Art was his religion.

In all cases, however, the truly religious person has to have certain qualities, whatever his creed or lack of it. Of these, probably the most outstanding is that of feeling awe and wonder, a sense of there being Mystery beyond anything he can apprehend; and together with this, love based on a sense of unity with

38

the world around him: an unemotional, unsentimental, undemanding love, which leaves each person free within that love.

Basically, Religion is thus the ladder which joins heaven and earth through its many rungs. Messengers or angels constantly run between the two kingdoms, agents of the noumenal Source of all things. It may be noted, too, that the latter says that He will bring Jacob *again* into a land which, presumably, and especially as the picture occurred in a dream, refers to a state of consciousness rather than to a geographical location. Jacob is to be once again related to the place from which he starts, if he listens to what his Essence tells him. This occurs by means of the angels who shuttle back and forth between the psychic world of dreams and the Essential one where God stands.

The myth sums up the principle of Religion in a very beautiful manner. But man, in the existential realm, would get lost without further help. He needs more explicit ideas from which to work. These are to be found in plenty all over the world and at all times, by the one who learns how to look for them. Frazer, in his monumental *Golden Bough,* gives us a vast amount of material from which it becomes clear that what Aldous Huxley later labelled "the Perennial Philosophy" is basically the same everywhere in the world. This philosophy becomes highly colored with local and racial ideas, but the root is the same in Polynesia or Christendom, in ancient Egypt and in modern days. The scriptures of India tell the same things as the Judaeo-Christian writings which treat of esoteric doctrine. The language of symbols is world-wide and goes far beyond and behind that of ordinary speech, so that a man like Jung tells of discussing profundities with an American Indian chief simply in terms of diagrams expressing the philosophical principles under examination.

Still more explicit were the rituals and forms which belonged to the Mystery schools. We do not know a great deal about what took place in the penetralia of the Temples, but in olden days there were great religious festivals and processions to which the uninitiated public were admitted, often as actual participants. Even in early Christianity, however, there were some things which were done in private, and only in the presence of the catechumens — baptized members, equivalent to the initiates of other Mystery groups. Still today the doors of the sanctuary are closed in Eastern Orthodox churches for the canon of the Mass and the consecration of the bread and wine. The Masonic fraternity equally preserves the idea of secrecy.

Clearly, Mystery schools, however valuable in their prime, lend themselves to all kinds of abuses when they become decadent. But what we know of their practices shows us that the rites inevitably rest on myth. This is so even if that myth becomes cluttered with what Mrs. Rhys Davids, the Buddhist scholar, referred to as "monkish accretions" — worship of idols, lists of saints and the rest of the things which obscure the simple creeds enunciated by all the great Teachers of Religion.

We owe to C. G. Jung the first clear study of the nature of myth and its place in the modern world. He opened out a whole new realm of meaning when he first discovered how, at a certain stage in analysis, patients began to have dreams and sometimes waking visions which made a profound impact on their minds; which "stayed with them" perhaps for years. He saw that when this happened, he was dealing with something expressed in the language of symbol and myth, which is also that of Religion. He found that, as it were, it grew out from inside the individual, and was not the result of reading and memory; that it was in a tongue belonging to people from all parts of the world and from all times. This was made all the more pointed when he met Richard Wilhelm the Sinologist, and read his translation of the ancient Chinese classic, *The Secret of the Golden Flower*. He found that the forms of the Mystery tradition were to be discovered in the depths of the modern, western, individual mind which probably had never so much as heard of this tradition. Hence, it followed that Religion (as distinct from religious forms and observances) was intrinsic to man, not an imposed superstition, and that Freud's pathetic attempts to dethrone all religion as wishful thinking failed to take into account the other-dimensionality of the mind as apart from the flat plane of materialism.

Jung carried matters further when he saw that when mythological images appeared in his patients' dreams they were then at a point where drastic and sometimes dramatic transformations might take place in their personalities. These changes went much deeper than those which occurred as a result of ordinary analysis into the past. The dream material carried a power of its own, a magic of the kind we learn about in the great legends of our race and even, in simpler and more naive form in popular fairy-tales. Winged horses, heroic figures, wizards and witches, not to mention enchanted swords and grails are of little avail, or would be if they existed, at the physical level. But in the mind they are as real and as powerful as any dreamer could wish. Myth is thus *psychic* truth, even if not within the bounds of physical possibility where it often seems like nonsense.

Further still, large-scale study tells us that, though myth has a certain consistency of language — a Chinese using much the same symbology as a modern American — it tends to spring into prominence in the life of a group at a moment of crisis or change, and into an individual's dreams when he too stands on the brink of a new phase of life or near to physical death. The language is the same, but the force of its impact is directed onto the group or the individual as the case may be.

Much has been written on this matter and need not be repeated here. But there is one aspect of it which concerns our own thesis about the difference between existential and Essential life. Jung used the term *archetype* or *archetypal image* when speaking of the content of myth. He himself realized the difference between these two terms, but he seems not to have emphasized it enough for many people to see it. Yet if we consider archetypes as the source of mythological material, it is important that we understand the way in which this source — in the Essential world — links onto the image or images of the existential realm, serving as ladders between the two.

The word *archetype* is derived from the Greek prefix which signifies a first or primal cause, as well as being used for *ancient* or in some such time-suggesting sense. The word is best taken for the numinous or abstract principle behind any thing or group of things in the phenomenal world. Being thus Numinous or Essential, it is not extended in space-time, but is what we would call a mathematical point with neither size nor time-extension. Like the point, it does not really exist, yet it is of immense importance. It has position, which gives it its dynamism, but it cannot be depicted in any way. It is, however, capable of reflecting itself into the dimensional world, to come into existence in terms of space and time. It is there as an *image* which depends on and reflects the archetype but it is not the archetype itself. God is said to have created the universe, an archetypal expression of Himself, but, as it says in the *Bhagavad-Gita*, "Having pervaded the universe with one fragment of Myself, I remain" — as the Supreme Archetype itself.

We may proceed from this to consider the nature of archetypes. They are the essential quality, the quiddity of anything: not the thing itself. They are "essential" in the Oxford Dictionary's sense, the "nature" of that thing: the "tree-ness" of every tree, the "cat-ness" of every cat, and so on. But we can also have archetypes of "conifer-ness" within the larger one of "tree-ness," or of "felinity" for all the cat tribe, over and above that of our domestic pets. We may remind ourselves here of what is said about Tao as being "there" at all levels and on all scales. The same can be said of archetypes, these occurring in a hierarchy such as "conifer-ness," "tree-ness," "vegetable-ness" and so on. The important thing is the fact that they represent Essence behind phenomena, and like the "peakness" of any experience, they are the summit and origin of a particular category of phenomena.

In trying thus to define what is almost indefinable, we have had to use the ordinary pattern of the mind and its language: that is, we have started from the concrete, existent object and worked toward the Essential. This is the human way of trying to understand things beyond our normal range. In fact, however, we must postulate the reverse, Nature proceeding from the Noumenal toward the phenomenal. The archetype, the "idea in the mind of God" comes first, the created object second. If this object is the result of man's intervention, i.e. an artefact, the concept or archetypal image follows from touch with a primal archetype. This is then elaborated at the existential level of the mind and the thing created becomes the final stage in the total action.

In this way, our minds have been working upstream, against the current of numinous life. This life flows outward or downward, whichever way we prefer to think, from the realm of Essence into that of phenomenal existence. In the ordinary mind, archetypes present themselves in images of a particular power, perceived subjectively as dreams and visions of heroic, mythical figures and symbols, of which Jacob's ladder is one example. Their power can be considered as being due to numinous forces playing through them; and as collective because, if we take a series of the dreams of an individual, we find in them the symbols of the universal language of world mythology. At the same time as they belong to mankind rather than to individual man, they have an individual aim, show the single man his own spiritual problems and the solution to them, if he will try to understand them and what they have to tell him. Individual man is an incarnation of his own archetype. He is his own myth. His spiritual task is to understand and live that myth before he can transcend it and pass beyond it into what lies beyond the human kingdom.

In speaking thus, it is not intended to imply that every one of us has to find himself in terms of a dramatic story such as we call myth. But it means that, in some form or another, he has to develop the pattern of his Essential individuality so that it fills and transforms his life. We have already mentioned the Indian dancer who felt that his Religion was in the perfection of the dance. Others find their way through other channels, artistic, social, creative in some way in the real sense of creation which is akin to that of the arts. For true creation inevitably connects with archetypal principles which express themselves through images or ideas in the polar world of existence.

The archetype is abstract, dimensionless, numinous. It *is*. In contrast to this, the images we see in our "big" dreams and visions represent existential, phenomenal projections of the archetype proper. In this way, when we dream of heroes, gods, daimons, in a drama in which also occur symbols such as the mandala, the serpent of wisdom, grails, spears, swords, etc., we are perceiving not the archetype but its existential reflection, extended in terms of space and time.

The image is dynamic and brings with it power and influence. This power is based in Essence, but when it descends into the realm of the personality, it follows the rule and becomes polarized. Every archetypal image is, if one goes deeply enough into it, dual, having a "light" and a "shadow" aspect. One without the other is incomplete. Thus there can be no *personal* God without a corresponding Devil, no saint without an anti-saint. The "devouring mother" so often quoted in psychological studies is the shadowy aspect of the beneficent, fertile and creative World-Mother, the warlock the negative of the Wise Old Man. The God who stands opposite the Devil, and who is worshipped in most churches is, of course, not the Supreme and Essential God, which is in no sense anthropomorphic. It (one cannot say "He" or "She") IS. The God-Devil pair *exists*. This is a matter of which some modern churchmen — Tillich, Robinson, Wren-Lewis, to mention them only — are becoming increasingly insistent.

To return now to the theme of individual man: his aim should be to try to become aware of the archetype behind any image, and this he seems to do when he follows the "light" aspect of it *while not ignoring or repressing the "shadow" side*. The latter represents the past, the former the future. So he names one evil, the other good — in themselves a *yin-yang* pair; so each one represents something incomplete. No man can know God who does not also know Satan; no man can know himself unless he also knows his own shadow. Jesus, the pattern of man on his way to super-humanity told Satan, in the desert, "Get thee behind me." This saying may have lost its impact in translations later than the Jacobean, but in the old form it shows us a profound truth: that a Man facing the light needs to have his shadow in its proper place, behind him. It also suggests that a man without a shadow is not real, he is only a ghost of his whole Being. It tells us also that to become integrated people, we need to seek beyond what we call the "good" and to look for numinous heavenly Goodness, where evil is absorbed and transformed by acceptance, and not repressed or denied. Here both light and shadow are merged into what in Egypt was sometimes described as the Dark Light, which is the Divine.

Myth, then, is a dramatized story which includes symbols. It is the Jacob's ladder which links the phenomenal world of our personal life with the spiritual level of our Being. But to climb that ladder requires the discipline of self-understanding, so that the personal message of any myth which touches us, whether from outside or from inside our minds, becomes apparent. It may be that religious forms which are real give this personal message, and valid rituals — myth expressed in dramatic form — may help, if only for a time. But they may also become something of a habit and, as has been said, obstacles in the way to true Religion; just as psychology of any particular school may come to stand in the way of full self-knowledge.

The power of myth and the symbols embodied in it are entirely real, even though "invisible" as that word is used in chapter 2. That power derives from the link with the actual and Essential archetype, and its effect is as great at its own level as is any physical phenomenon at its own, where matter is changed or moved. The level at which myth operates is that of the psyche, the existential mind; and here, denoting as it does, a movement from within the depths of an individual toward the more superficial levels of himself — those in which he spends his daily life, his existence — it affects the whole pattern of his integrated wholeness. It does not matter that what the myth tells is physically impossible — one may take as an example such a dogma as the physical ascension of the Virgin. Its truth lies in what it denotes as a mental need of an individual or a collective group, and has to be seen and accepted as such, even though its physical interpretation makes nonsense of it. Myth is psychic or psycho-spiritual truth, not physical fact.

In this connection, a friend of the writers suggests a line of thought which is worth following up. This is that, at times in human history, myth may well spill out further than the psychic or mental realm, and become coincident with historical, time-occurring events. She cites not only the Gospel story, but also the legends of such persons as King Arthur, Charlemagne and others some of whom, at least, are known historical characters, but around whom myth has gathered. Mind, as we know both from parapsychological research and from daily life, directly or indirectly affects the physical world. It does so directly, it appears, from still somewhat inconclusive experiments in psycho-kinesis. It does so indirectly and constantly when thought and feeling on the part of individual or group bring about physical changes and events.

It seems possible therefore that numinous, archetypal forces may sometimes manifest in physical history. The Gospel story — for which so eminent a thinker as Albert Schweitzer could find no *historical* evidence — might therefore have taken place

45

exactly as described. King Arthur may have been more than a rough tribal chieftain, and may have gathered about him a group of idealistic knights living in a Camelot which would have been, and may indeed be found to be, a most crude and un-romantic place. In any case, the importance of these characters lies in their mythological nature, in the forces brought to bear through them on the minds of those around them, either at the time or even today. The history, if such it be, is entirely second-ary to the myth in importance.

This reality brings us to another principle, the power of belief. Shakespeare (Hamlet, Act II, Sc. 2) tells us that "There is nothing good or bad but thinking makes it so." It would be absurd to think that he was, in saying this, anticipating the find-ings of modern parapsychology; but it seems to indicate that he realized the potency of thought and feeling in their dynamic, creative or destructive effects. Our minds make things into what we believe them to be. The classical Hindu example of a man seeing a stick and mistaking it for a poisonous snake and acting accordingly comes to mind: he mentally "created" a snake out of a harmless piece of wood, until he realized his mistake, when the tension dropped.

When it comes to bringing myth, or thought about numin-ous, archetypal principles to bear on physical objects, the po-tency of our normal mind becomes enhanced by that of the archetypal image. An object may thus become charged, as it were, with the power of that archetypal idea. It is, using this word widely, "transubstantiated," even if the "accidents" or outer matter remain what they have always been. This would explain the difficulty which is often found in the non-Catholic toward the one who accepts the idea that a piece of bread and some grape-juice, fermented or not, becomes something very special during the Mass. If one were to examine the consecrated elements, they would show starch grains, water, sugar, gluten, etc. just as much after consecration as before. But because of the faith of the believer, and the archetypal roots of the sym-bolism, they would, *at a non-physical level,* have been changed in line with the belief of the Church.

It has to be admitted that, whatever their personal beliefs, many sensitive people feel a difference between a church where the Sacrament is reserved and one where it is not — an observation based on extra-sensory perception but not of necessity of anything more elevated or spiritual.

Perhaps the most troublesome aspect of the whole question of myth and symbol lies in the duality of the images. We have already touched on this but it deserves further attention. Man is essentially dual in his mind. He is, to use our phrases, both "instinctive" and "essential." It is out of this that the pairs of opposites we call good and evil arise. We are, as a species, basically schizophrenic, and the form of psychosis we label by that name is — as in the case of every disease — only an exaggeration of normality beyond a certain point.

Essential man has to learn to accept both sides of himself, but this does not mean that he has to give way to retrograde forces. Like Jesus, he has to get them into the right place in his total economy, where they will serve a useful purpose and cease from being a detriment to him. Hugh l'Anson Fausset, in *The Flame and the Light,** calls the instinctive energies, upwelling from the earth, as it were, the Flame, the energy which drives the human psyche. But it has to become integrated with the Light, the guiding spiritual, teleological urges, if man is to be complete. Both are needed in order to reach consciousness of Essence. One alone will not be enough.

This situation is exemplified in what was either a dream or a "hypnogogic image" where a man saw himself standing on the edge of a pool, looking at his own image reflected in the water. The figure was, obviously, upside down. He found himself saying to it in his dream, "You are my opposite number. What I love you hate, what I hate you love. Your good is my evil, my evil your good. In every way we are opposites. *But you are part of myself,* and therefore I must love you." The impression was so vivid, he said, that for the next few days he felt himself to be constantly accompanied by this "Dweller on the Threshold," a term he borrowed from occultism; that whenever he put a foot to the ground, another foot came up, sole to sole, against his. Within a short time, he found himself face to face with a shadow situation which filled him with horror and dismay but which, when he eventually found his way through, brought

*Abelard-Schuman, London.

47

him out a different person. His love for his own shadow-self did not in any way mean giving way to his passions. It involved his facing and not rejecting it any longer, so that it became integrated with him, and gave him new energy and purpose, and better balance in daily life.

*   *   *

An entirely different approach to the archetypal images and the archetypes themselves, is to be obtained from Paul Tillich, the late "existentialist theologian" and, as he himself said, "protestant." He argued that if, in religion or any other human activity, we attributed ultimate value to things which are not ultimate, we created idolatry; we "demonized" our outlook. His "protest," he said, took the form of constantly refusing to agree to idolatry, and reminding people of the need to seek the real ultimate God. The person who deals only with archetypal *images,* however exalted, fails to look for the Ultimate or Essential, and so casts a shadow over his consciousness. The archetype — and the Absolute or Supreme God is the basic, or final Archeytpe in which all lesser archetypes originate and are resolved — is what we need constantly to seek in order to reach our human goal.

Archetypal symbols, as embodied in myth, serve as a ladder toward the heaven up to which Jacob's reached. They are not themselves heavenly or Essential. That is why, in Zen and Taoist philosophy, the disciple is told that there comes a time when, having reached the top rung of the ladder of discipline and observances, he must kick the ladder away and go on mounting without it. But first the ladder needs to be surmounted, in whatever form it presents itself to us. Myth is, for western man today, perhaps one of the most immediate and present forms of that ladder. It is not the only one. To use it constructively, however, it needs to become personal, individual, an intrinsic part of one's mental make-up. It is entirely valid for people to take part in external forms of worship or sacramental practices, which, as we have said, are the expression of myth. But the need today is to realize that if one does so — and it is basically not necessary that anybody should take part in congregational forms of worship — the deeper values have to be found within oneself, and convey to one some personal meaning. This en-

48

larges understanding and raises consciousness above its ordinary mundane level and leads eventually to the permanent illumination which is the goal of human fulfillment.

Chapter VIII

THE GREAT WHEEL

There is in the major religions of the world a concept which is perhaps most clearly stated in the Hindu idea of there being two paths in human life, one that of outgoing, the other that of return. Precisely the same idea is expressed in the Christian parable of the Prodigal Son, where a young man leaves home, travels widely and eventually comes back to a great welcome. A Gnostic document, the *Hymn of the Robe of Glory,* amplifies this parable and gives it more detail and an emphasis different from that in our own version of the scriptures; for it does not suggest that he comes back as a repentant sinner, which is a later gloss and probably a mistranslation to suit the puritanical trends of Jacobean times. On the contrary, on his return the young man receives from his father a Robe of Glory, as a reward for his achievement in bringing home the Pearl of Great Price — also mentioned by St. Matthew. That Pearl may be taken as wisdom, the flowering of Selfhood, the achievement of Self-consciousness in its fullest sense, or in any other way which suggests that the Prodigal has become spiritually mature. In contrast, the stay-at-home brother is ignored. He is still the ignorant youth, in the state in which both brothers were before the less amenable set out on the path of existence from his home in Being. It may be added that the name of the Prodigal may well have been Adam, or Adam-Eve, though in the story of the latter only the first part is told. In any case, the journey is circular, bringing the traveller back to the point from which he started, but with an all-important difference in himself.

We are here reminded of the universal symbol typified by

the *mandala* of the East, and by the *ouroboros,* or serpent with its tail in its mouth. As with Tao, moreover, there are endless cycles, one within the other, alongside one another, overlapping one another, on all scales.

In the overall picture, we are shown the myth of man. His evolution is, as is everything in nature, cyclic. That which is latent stirs, becomes projected from its sleeping state into existence. There it awakes and develops until it is ready to return Home.

The outgoing phase is that where instinctive man drives the roots of germinated individuality into the soil of the animal mind. The phase of return is that where, like any plant, this germ starts to grow mainly upward toward sun and air. Here alone it can blossom and fruit. Like the plant, however, man must preserve and even feed his roots if he is not to wither away, a thing sometimes forgotten in the enthusiasm felt by some for the spiritual Vision.

The transition from one stage to the next is, in a literal sense, a conversion, a change of direction, ultimately through 180 degrees, toward the point of departure. It is often, in the life of an individual, a period of conflict and difficulty. He is not, as it were, gathered up entirely at a point on the evolutionary trail, but part of him is ahead and has entered the Essential phase, while the rest lags behind in the instinctive phase. It is now that the pull between the two becomes most acute, and also the moment when true Religion comes into the picture. This is when, were he Jacob, he would have his dream. The emphasis on the word *true* is necessary because so much religious thought is at the polarized level rather than at the Essential level, and merely serves to stress the conflict without resolving it. It does not help to speak of oneself as a "miserable sinner" and to say there is "no health in me," if one says at the same time that man is a child of God, hence something more than sinful and mortally sick, then to ask God to change one when nobody but oneself can make the change. Those who have experienced the Vision know that this is so, and that only their own effort will carry them safely round the lower arc of the circle of life.

It is difficult for those who have the "intimations of immortality" to find outside help in expanding these intimations.

51

If they turn to the churches and temples, they are apt to find these wanting, for most have been debased into something which is, except in name, pure materialism. They call for spirituality but reject the personal and instinctive as evil without seeing it as the spiritual expression in its earlier phase.

Yet Religion, in its truer and more numinous form, far from treating the urge to establish ourselves firmly in the material world as due to innate sinfulness, realizes it as a first step in spiritual development. In a crude way, some say that if you do not "sin" you cannot ever be absolved and so be "saved." This seems to have been Rasputin's doctrine, and he practised it to the full. The intuitive basis of this exaggeration is valid, provided we see well enough what religious teachers and writers remind us: that there is behind the urge into matter the teleology which eventually — and, in fact, all the time — draws us back toward the Essential ground behind our existence. In the Roman Church, some of the Lenten Litanies thank God for the "necessary Fall of Adam": without a Fall there could be no Redemption. In another form, it is said that man can only live both "from Heaven above and from Earth beneath," a theme worked out very fully in Hugh l'Anson Fausset's *The Flame and the Light*.

If these propositions are valid, they involve a number of questions into which we do not propose to enter, but which it is well to bear in mind. For it is clear that a span of a mere seventy years is not enough to cover the whole of necessary existential experience. A man may be serene and die happily after a full life, but, however saintly, it is still obvious that only the very rarest individual has liquidated his material life enough to be called one of the elect; or, as Buddhism would put it, to be free from the Wheel of Rebirth and pass into Nirvana or Heaven. This suggests that liberation into pure Being is likely to require more than one cycle of incarnation in the existential world. The idea of reincarnation is widespread and explicit enough in the East; one can dismiss the notion that a man can ever regress into inhabiting an animal body as unlikely both on psychological and physiological grounds. Strange as it may seem, too, and despite the denials of theological students, reincarnation is in no way contrary to the teachings of Christianity. Indeed, until Gnosticism was denounced, it was part of general Christian

52

doctrine; and others besides Dr. Leslie Weatherhead have seen passages in the Bible, and even in the Gospels, which appear to take reincarnation for granted.

To close this chapter, here is a brief examination of what the ultimate state at the end of the Cycle is likely to be for man. The idea of Heaven or Paradise is general, but in its debased forms gives us a picture of something clearly derived from the instinctive, desire-filled aspect of ourselves. In contrast to this we have what seems to be the purest, and most likely, exposition of what happens when man, fully self-realized and perfected, completes the journey, passes out of the "middle state" and off the narrow "isthmus" into the wide lands beyond.

Nirvana is said to be this end. The word means "extinction." But, to quote Sir Edwin Arnold's *The Light of Asia,*

> If any teach Nirvana is to cease,
> Say unto such they lie.
> If any teach Nirvana is to live,
> Say unto such they err; not knowing this,
> Nor what light shines beyond their broken lamps,
> Nor lifeless, timeless bliss.

This precisely states the Buddhist doctrine, in the language of paradox and the contradictions which are the mark of the polarized mental world when it encounters Essence.

We may ask, in practical terms, what it all means, what is extinguished, what is it that neither lives nor dies? The Buddhist whose mind is clear as to the real doctrine, uncluttered by "monkish accretions," will reply that what dies is the *mayavic,* illusory or false idea of self-identity, the personal psychological ego, built up out of the mind, its memories, associations, desires. What remains? Essential Self-identity as we glimpse it in moments of real insight. The ego is self-in-separation working in the field of the mind we know. Self is Self-in-Union, functioning in a different kind of mind which is universal and hence infinite.

In terms of this book this state means that the human being has now passed from the world of existence into that of Being. He is free *from* the former but, if tradition is to be believed, he is also free *of* it: he can enter it or not as he,

53

from his superior position in consciousness decides. The realm of "opposites," of *yin* and *yang,* are his to command, and they hold no secrets for him. The Wheel of the Law has not ceased to turn, but its turning is no longer any concern of his because he is now one with that Law. In other words, he has now reached the end of ordinary human evolution and is ready to pass on into that mysterious future which at once lies beyond humanity and at the same time is latently present with us all the time.

Chapter IX

CYCLES AND PERIODICITY

Scientific observation tends to confirm the view that everything in the universe runs in cycles. These may not always be obvious because they overlap, they may contain smaller cycles, or be themselves contained in larger ones. Sometimes, moreover, the time element is on so vast or small a scale that it is virtually beyond measure. On the small scale, we know that some phenomena last a millionth of a second, but there is no reason for thinking there may not be even briefer ones.* On the larger scale, we have the universe, which has been observed in a state of expansion to which there is no foreseeable end. But if there is any truth in the Hindu idea of "the Day and Night of Brahma," it seems as if the cosmos itself, as it is today, is in one phase of its life, preceded and followed by others, equally long, where it might be seen to shrink. If this is so, it would show that the cyclic principle is universal. It fits in, moreover, with the idea of the "big bang" which, when the matter of the universe condensed enough, would result in a vast nuclear explosion which would set the expansive phase into action again.

A complication is that cyclic action does not of necessity take place in terms of time. In a given chemical system it is possible for, let us say alkalinity, to grow up to a point where it would cease on its own to increase, and be replaced by a new state where some other process would follow, leading to re-acidification, this in turn to be followed by a return to alkalinity.

---

*This, it has been suggested, may eventually prove untrue. The argument points out that the universe may be everywhere divided into quanta and that just as we have *photons*, we may eventually discover *"chronons."*

Another image for the same thing is that of the pendulum. Its action shows us what is called periodicity, the same as cyclic movement, but uncoiled, as it would be if a new factor — time, for instance — were combined with cyclic recurrence. The simplest mathematical representation of periodicity is the "sine curve," the regularly rising and falling line along a given axis. The part above the axis may be called *yang,* the part below, *yin,* the axis itself showing us the Tao. It does not matter, therefore, whether we speak in terms of cycles or periods: they represent the same rhythmic pattern.

The simple graph, however, is not adequate to show us a life-pattern except perhaps for the most mechanical and uncomplicated entities. Other rhythms play into and weave around the basic one and make highly complex figures. The phases of the moon, for instance, clearly play upon the woman's body, where there are also such cycles as the heart-beat, breathing, and so on. But so do the seasons, the year and endless other cyclic forces both earthy and subtler, affect her. Her total graph would therefore be a very complicated figure. So, of course, would be that of a male, and of every other creature.

Here the Taoists have philosophically and scientifically long been ahead of the west. As Jung tells us, western science is, or has been, that of causality spread out along the time-track; but in the east science has concentrated on the immediate moment, concerned with the synthetic pattern and significance of what is immediately around one. The *I-Ching*, or *The Book of Changes* is a deeply significant treatise on the inter-combination of *yin* and *yang* rhythms impinging on any instant in time and therefore creating an immediate pattern for life and conduct. Those who make serious use of the book say they find it a very useful guide in important problems.

Viewed from a state of consciousness beyond the limitations of the ordinary mind, ebb and flow, cyclic change, or the swing of a pendulum anchored in eternity, would be seen to be the law.

This is probable enough for us to be able to think of humanity and the development of its consciousness in the same terms. Historians, it is true, have failed to find any kind of order in events such as battles, invasions, the rise and fall of empires and cultures. But it may be that this is because they give undue importance to physical events. Humanity's history is focused in the mind and, moreover, the place where mental development is most active moves from one geographical locality to another. This may be only because of the tendency of the mental climate of an old civilization embedded in tradition and habit, to hamper new mental growth, so that it has to find its outlet elsewhere.

So far, moreover, the trend has been geographically from east to west. But today, not only has the main focus of progress caught up with itself round the world, it extends more and more in every direction over the globe. This means that the cultural patterns which are emerging today are more general and universal and less colored by purely local habits and traditions. The Japanese, Chinese, Indian, European and other local patterns tend either to die out — to our loss — or to become subsidiary to new modes of thought, whether these be in science, religion, art, or in the lower cultural levels of cheap music and meretricious arts and crafts. If a balance between ancient and modern could be established, it would result in something which would place before people a sense of their roots in their own traditions and myths. It would also show a progressive movement toward the unity of the human species throughout the world in one complex cultural entity. At the present time, unfortunately, uprooting is more in evidence than constructive growth.

In terms not of space but of time, certain rhythms seem to be obvious when we take a long term view of global history at the mental level. One of these is seen in the alternation of the major religions between a form of quiet introversion and one where external observances and rites are advocated. Hinduism — complex, multiple and inchoate, yet having a general flavor of its own — is popularly concerned with temple worship. Buddhism then says, "Study the Law, dispel ignorance" and in its pure forms, reduces observances to a minimum. Christianity returns to ritual. Today, a form of in-turned quietism seems once again to be gaining ground. Islam, rising in the same locality as Judaism, contrasts with it. It is active, propagandist; the Jewish faith self-enclosed. Islam is opposed to images and the use of objects in worship; Judaism pays much attention to having the right ritual materials if not the "graven images," leaving it to Christianity to fill this need for many worshippers.

These generalizations are obviously open to question, and exceptions can be found all along the line. But careful analysis tends to show that these are a matter of smaller cyclic stages within the greater ones, as Protestanism is within the wider Christian era.

For our purposes, however, the interesting thing is the alternation between a stage of stability and conservatism and one in which movement predominates, representing a swing between polar opposites in the mind and thought of people. The relics of the past exemplify this right up to the present day. It takes only a glance to see the four-square staticism of ancient Egyptian statues and buildings. This suggests that, as in India, we have one form of culture. In Greece we feel the buildings and the best of its sculpture as dynamic and living, in a sense moving all the time. China, too, seems to have something of this dynamism in many of its forms. In the Middle Ages, "primitive" art, exquisite as it is, had not the fluid quality of that of the Renaissance. And today we can find a contrast between the wonder of a Gothic cathedral and such a building as the chapel built by Le Corbusier at Ronchamps, in France, where there is not a straight line or a plain surface, or any symmetry in placing windows, and where one feels the quality of wave and wind in motion.

In our examples, it seems that we have spoken of the phenomena of greater and lesser phases. Christian culture is on a larger scale than Medievalism and the Renaissance, Victorianism and modern trends. What matters, however, is that we see the alternation, and the relation between stages in terms of the polarity expressed in China as the *yin* or feminine, conservative, preservative, static, as against the dynamism of the masculine *yang* principle. If we see this, not only do certain things occurring today become more comprehensible, they also show the lines which may help to bring about change in a positive and not a negative direction.

It seems clear that we are now moving into a dynamic stage. In every sphere of life there is change, not merely in the outer field, but much deeper below the surface. The new quality of modern culture, insofar as it has yet acquired a semblance of shape, is away from the static and towards dynamic interplay between .complementary elements. Science has lost its categorical dogmatism. It plays with uncertainty, probability, randomness. Matter has become nebulous in that, like energy-waves, at one time looked upon as the opposite of atoms, it can be thought of by the same mind as consisting of particles or as energy without becoming involved in contradictions. In Christianity there is much more acceptance of ideas which, a few centuries ago, would have resulted in the burning as heretics of the bishops and others who voice them today. In philosophy, similar plasticity tends to replace the heavy cut-and-dried metaphysics of the last century. In art we have gone beyond impressionism into fields which, presumably, stand for something, or out of which something new will emerge. The one thing certain is that it will not be of the order of what we have seen in the past.

Perhaps, moreover, things today seem much more chaotic than at other times of change because of the coincidence of a minor and a major cycle operating in the same general direction. The forces are therefore even more disruptive and powerful than at less critical times in the larger course of human evolutionary history. In principle, however, the basic rule holds good, and can perhaps be understood best in terms of the poles. We shall at this point again use the Chinese names rather than the western ones, so as to avoid too narrow a meaning. Our association with such words as positive and negative, masculine and feminine — lesser classes within the more universal concepts of *yin* and *yang* — can only serve to confuse.

Within the stable, static forms we have already suggested as being *yin*, we need to see, as always, *yin-yang* polarity. But here the poles tend to be separated, as it were, frozen. But in the *yang* phase, these forces are free and moving. When they harmonize, we have an interplay, an interweaving between them. If they are not so harmonized we have chaos, rebellion, revolution and destruction. Conservative culture finds its stability in the first. The dynamic phase owes its stability to the kind of movement we find in a spinning top, in an aircraft flying steadily through an unstable element, in the difference between the jet engine depending on a draft of gas and the one moved by pistons where the energy supply is enclosed in a box.

We find, also, that modern culture once more gives a place to the feeling aspects of our minds. Science, at one time, tried to eliminate feeling and to deal in pure reason. There is today something of a rebellion against giving rationality entire dominance in our judgments. The feeling-intuitive aspect of life is now realized as essential to full understanding. Yet if we equate intellect and thought with the *yang* pole, and feeling with *yin,* we find ourselves faced with the kind of paradoxes which are the mark of the dynamic culture which belongs to the future, if not of the present. For, looked at from another angle, thought tends to the orderliness and stability of *yin,* while feeling dynamizes and energizes the intellect, hence must be *yang.* (Eve was the one who, in Eden, stirred Adam into action: a woman, and hence *yin* in her outer aspect, but with *yang* potent on the inside. These poles are reversed in Adam).

Enough has been said to suggest both that evolution runs in cycles, and also that the transition from one to another is apt to be extremely confusing both to the onlooker and to the historian looking back. This is all the more so when the movement is from stable to unstable, from a static to a moving phase, because contradictions and inconsistencies abound. Moreover, in a stable society individuals are invited to accept external tradition and authority, which the Christian churches still do, whereas in the moving phase, individuals are thrown back on themselves, to find their security at the center of their Being. Truth is not in the forms and words of scriptures or rituals or the dogmas of religion, whether in its ancient creeds or in the modern one of science, but *behind* these, in the realm of myth and archetype: in Tao. Hence individual man comes to the fore as the source of his own deeper insights. He is also the focus from which he may help order to emerge from chaos through his inner contact with Being or Tao, his true Self — the God within.

Chapter X

GOOD AND EVIL

This chapter is not intended to be in any way moralistic. The problem of good and evil can be discussed in pragmatic terms based on the philosophy of Being and existence without emulating the people who so constantly tell us what God wants, how to behave, and what to believe. A much more realistic approach can be found and, indeed, is necessary. It is not conceivable, moreover, that anybody seriously interested in Essential problems should be unconcerned with such an approach, particularly where their own lives are involved.

In a wider context, it is doubtful whether, in Nature, a dichotomy exists between good and evil. The forces of the elements, the apparent cruelty of animals, and many other aspects of prehuman life are not either good or evil: they are simply part of the great pattern of the world. But when the human ego enters the field, there is almost immediately a split between two aspects of natural life: that which holds to the past and that which represents movement forward toward the future. It is this which, in its effect on the human personality, leads to "the knowledge of good and evil," the fruit of the Tree through which man became man, that is, man became ethical and moral.

The two terms, in early stages, virtually coincide. But where we are today, it is well to distinguish in principle between them, though both in Greek and in English, they are usually treated as almost interchangeable. *Moral* is derived from the Latin *mores* or customs. To be moral suggests, therefore, to conform to standards accepted by the community. This may well be allowed to stand. But *ethics* will be a term better used for our purposes as a code applied to the individual. That the two standards usually coincide is evident from the similarity of accepted meaning, but as we study self-conscious man, emerging from mass consciousness, he should discover for himself what is right *for him* even if it does not altogether tally with what the community as a whole believes.

First, it will be useful if we define good and evil, a matter which, in terms of evolutionary philosophy, is really simple. That is good which advances evolution and, in the case of man, leads to greater awareness and understanding; that is evil which retards evolution, and in particular, since the whole concept is a product of man's thought, whatever diminishes his individuality, his awareness and his freedom of mental choice.

Modern depth psychology has outlined a useful view of the development of a moral sense, one which, up to the turning point which was discussed in a previous chapter, is also ethical. After that, morals and ethics may diverge at least to some extent.

According to Freud, the human ego finds itself between two opposing forces. There is the *id* or *libido,* the impersonal instinctive urge, which seeks fulfillment, pleasure, satisfaction for the individual. On the other side are the forces of social pressure which urge conformity to accepted moral standards. These too operate at the level of instinct, in the sense that individual safety lies in being "in" with the herd and not outcast. There is therefore satisfaction, "pleasure," in being moral. Since the two forces seek different immediate ends, conflict easily arises, and when this becomes too strong, neurosis results.

Theoretically, social pressures distort the individual's freedom of expression. But the ego does not exist in isolation, only in the context of others of its kind, so the "super-ego," to use the technical term, though derived from the environment, must also be considered as an intrinsic part of the personality. "Cure" of neurosis occurs when some kind of truce is reached between the divided instinctive forces so that the ego is not pulled apart between them.

This is what most people achieve. When they develop to a certain age, they learn to conform and are reasonably content. Some, however, and the number seems to be growing constantly today, refuse to fit in and become rebels. They believe that, by so doing, they are setting themselves free. In reality, however, the quest for freedom to be what they call *themselves,* by rebellion, reveals personalities which are in every way as much enslaved by super-egoic morality as the conformists. Only, the reaction is in reverse.

This briefly, and doubtless over-simply, outlines the Freudian doctrines at any rate in their older form. Freud's main successor in the field was C. G. Jung who, without rejecting Freud's view, carried matters very much further. He added to his philosophy Alfred Adler's emphasis on the ego and its search for a place in the sun; but he then discovered that it was possible, even for the neurotic, to bring about a real resolution rather than a working compromise, between the libido and the super-ego, if the solution were sought *within the field of the ego itself.* This means that the ego has to discover how to move in another direction than that between libido and super-ego. Self-identity needs to change its character and its level of awareness in the direction of Being, even if it is a long way from actually operating there. Essential or numinous forces filter through into the levels where instinct has hitherto been dominant, and the total pattern of the individual changes and becomes more harmonious. It is as this occurs that ethics, in our sense, begins to overshadow or, better, to illumine morals.

At this point we need to remind ourselves that the very concept of good and evil represents a polarized pair, and so belongs to the level of existence, not to that of unitary Being. It cannot be otherwise. Yet it is evident that if movement toward Essential consciousness is what is required from the point of view of the evolutionary stream, the idea of goodness must have meaning beyond the one based on the horizontal plane of polarized opposites. This makes the problem very difficult to envisage with our ordinary mental habits, and still more so to explain. It seems as if, taking the expansion of consciousness as rising from the earth to the heavenly heights, one had to see the poles of good and evil one *above* the other. The one we call *good* is at the level of Being, the other below it, in the field of the personal, the instinctive, the evolutionary past. So it becomes necessary to conceive of there being, as well as a personal good, an Essential Good of which the personal good is a reflection, much as the ego eventually is seen as a reflection of the spiritual Self.

In other words, the goodness associated with the super-ego is capable of reflecting Essential Good, while it may also have a false face where what is good, in the sense of being satisfying and comfortable is, in reality, expediency. This is the avoidance of stress between the libido-energized aspect of the ego and that which desires to fit in with the collective mass of society. The need of the self-aware and would-be independent person is the Herculean task of discovering what is really Good and ethical, and to separate it from that which is moral without being in a real sense good.

We have suggested, when speaking of causality and of the interaction of *yin-yang,* that the polarity of one might change from positive to negative, or vice versa when a new relationship arises between that polar object and something else. In electricity, a carbon rod is said to be positive to one of zinc, in a battery. But negative zinc, in turn, might be positive to something else in another type of battery with a different electrode. We must therefore allow that, in the field of good and evil, what is good and forward-moving may at a later time become frustrating and so be evil, if only for a time and in a given context. To give an example, it may be that celibacy is good up to the time of marriage, but in a marriage it is likely to cause endless trouble and distortion, hence becomes evil.

There is thus no absolute existential standard of good and evil, a matter often not realized by the moralist. He encourages people to fuse ultimate Good and the super-ego. The depth psychologist is left with the task of separating the two so that true ethics emerge. This is a major problem for many people even if they do not fall within the category of the neurotic. It nevertheless becomes imperative, especially when trying to realize oneself, to learn to distinguish between behavior at the personal level which is in accord with Essential Goodness, and when it is merely dictated by slavery to the morality imposed by the mass. By analogy, one person's real good may carry him in a direction diametrically opposite to another's though he is also engaged on the same quest. A train entering a tunnel from one end finds emergence into the light at the opposite end from that of another coming from the other direction. What matters is that each finds the light, which is the same at either end. It may be added that a tunnel which is not open at both ends is not a way from place to place but a grave.

The individual who becomes aware of his true standard of what is Good finds himself free. His super-ego has been resolved, he no longer fears ostracism from outside and no longer has an inner sense of guilt. His moral code is also his ethical one and he can live freely and happily in society without feeling that in so doing he is hemmed in and his life pattern distorted.

This does not, however, mean that the well adjusted person becomes inactive and passive. On the contrary, he may at times feel that vigorous action is needed in order to live up to his code. He may discover that there are abuses, injustices which call for reform. But whereas the rebel is, in effect, reacting at the personal level, the well-found man *acts* rather than *re*acts. The focus from which his acts spring is at a level higher than the personal, and is based in a deeper vision of the need for reform than that of the reactive rebel who, only too often, over-compensates externally against an inner unresolved conflict. The aggressiveness of the self-styled pacifist is a very obvious example of this. The war-like tendencies which the person has and dislikes in his own mind, whether he is conscious of them or not, and about which he feels guilt, are used to attack in a highly bellicose manner the thing he consciously rejects. Many other examples of the same thing can be found in the sphere of reformers of all kinds.

An illustration of the true, non-reactive reformer, may be taken from the Gospels, where Jesus, on the Mount — always a symbol of a high level of consciousness, a "peak" — preached non-resistance to evil. A little later he scourged the money-changers in the Temple they were defiling. One can, it is true, take this story as showing how the uncrucified Jesus had human frailties, but it can indicate also how positive action may be taken without hatred or malice against the offenders. This, in theory, is the background of the impersonal administration of justice in a Court of Law, where vindictiveness and prejudice are supposed to be entirely absent. It is the "inaction in action" of the *Bhagavad-Gita* and other religious classics.

In this way, many of the social and political problems of the day come to be seen as a direct result of conflict both within the individual and in the collective mass of mankind. They reflect particularly the urge of the ego to free itself from false moralities;

but, unable as yet to discover a genuine ethical standard from which action should spring, it is apt to fall into a morass of good intentions resting on a false conception of what real freedom means. The result is that many causes, basically good in themselves, become the playground of the stresses within our confused minds. The right thing is advocated from the wrong level by people often in violent conflict in themselves, whether or not they are aware of it, and who find a means of exteriorizing that conflict in becoming reformers. They are reacting, not acting directly from a place of conscious understanding, and so spoil what might be truly constructive and good. This would not happen if we had resolved the war between our own moral sense and our individual ethical standard; and the reforms would be much more effective, instead of calling up resentment and ridicule, which only add to the discord in our world.

Chapter XI

MANA AND CHARISMA

One often hears the phrase "a magnetic personality" applied to certain people. They may be quite obscure from an outer point of view, not especially distinguished by expertise in a particular field, or knowledgeable, or skillful; but they seem to carry something with them which, especially in emergency, makes people turn to them as leaders or counsellors. They are influential without being domineering or otherwise trying to claim power; they may be humble workers in minor positions; yet it is as if they had an extra charge of psychic energy which impresses more than any superior knowledge or position in society. A district nurse, servant of her medical superiors, may in this way be a better "healer" than the man or woman armed with diplomas or degrees; the simple priest more respected than his bishop; the mob leader may be an uneducated peasant.

In the language of depth psychology, we would use the term Jung has taken from the Polynesian language, and call them *mana*. This is a useful word for which western tongues have no exact equivalent, though both the Indians and the Arabs have similar ones. It indicates an individual who has particular power, who influences others without trying necessarily to do so, though he may, at his own peril, use that power for his own ends, perhaps for evil rather than good. The malevolent witch doctor, the saintly priest, the film star or "pop" singer who exploits excessive sexuality, are all, in these terms, *mana*. So is the one who becomes the dictator of his country. But there is a vast difference between *mana* personalities when the personal ego of the individual becomes inflated, proud and vainglorious, and the impersonal quality of the truly saintly person.

It seems useful therefore to suggest that *mana* may occur at two levels, with different characteristics. These coincide with the over-sharp division made for purposes of discussion, between the levels of Being and existence, further explained in the relation between the archetype itself and the image of that archetype projected into the world of existence. The archetype is unitary and is beyond the realm of the personal. The image, on the other hand, is dual, has positive and negative polarity, and belongs to the personal, existential aspect of the mind.

Mana, as we shall use the term, is at the latter level and arises from identification with one or other side of the duality. Hence it opposes the other pole. Moreover, it is found at the level of the personal ego; whence the validity of the warning in Jolande Jacobi's book, *The Psychology of Jung.* For if the ego becomes inflated by the forces flowing through the image, it tends to be carried away by them for lack of the compensating, balancing effect of the rejected complementary power of the other pole. The result is apt to be fanaticism and self-importance.

If, on the other hand, the individual has, by whatever legitimate means, made contact with the archetype itself, touched the level of Being where Self is found, the numinous forces which flow through into his ordinary mind are balanced, not in conflict with one another. Hence they are doubly potent. This order of *mana* we will call, for convenience by the fashionable name, *charisma,* which is much the same as the "grace" of which theologians speak.

The *mana* personality, hence, is in danger. We have seen the vanity and strutting of dictators in our own time, the self-importance and narcissism of the popular actor, of the evangelist who, identified with one aspect of the existential god-devil pair, thinks of himself as a chosen messenger. If matters go too far, loss of judgment and mental balance develop; deterioration of the whole personality sets in, and the individual is likely to become a paranoiac. This happens regardless of whether the cause he advocates is "good" or not. If the individual is not sufficiently aware of himself to contain the forces playing through him, they gather momentum and run riot.

The charismatic person, making of him for discussion purposes one who has reached a very full degree of Self-realization, is quite a different type. He is essentially unassuming, very probably, though not necessarily, out of the public eye, unknown — as was Jacob Boehme, a great mystic, in his life time, a simple cobbler. He radiates a certain impersonal quality which evokes a response from any sensitive person who comes into contact with him; charisma emanates from a place beyond sexual differences. He IS what he is, without show or ostentation, makes no claims for himself to any kind of spiritual exaltation. He may or may not speak to a person, but those who come into his presence and are capable of responding to what he offers undergo a catalysis, an alchemical change, which may bring the conflicting elements in himself to a synthesis or resolution. He is sometimes a genuine worker of miracles — not the much-vaunted and advertised kind so often claimed by people who may or may not be merely *mana*, but those occurring quietly, silently, and possibly showing only in a subjective, inner change in the individual who benefits from it. Sometimes even gross physical disease is cured when, by all the laws of medicine and physiology, it should not be. Jesus, as shown us in the Gospels, was clearly such a one, and there are others on varying scales.

The charismatic person need not be highly intellectual or educated. Indeed, he may be scarcely literate, but, however inarticulate, he is intelligent about life as many intellectuals are not. He has an innate sense of meaning and value which expresses itself in the ability to stand in awe before the transcendental, and to love deeply and impersonally. Unlike the *mana* person, he is, moreover, unconscious of his power. As Krishnamurti says, one is not truly loving if one is aware of oneself as loving. Love IS. The *feeling* of loving is in the existential field. In some measure such a person may be said to incarnate the archetype itself, including both the light and dark aspects which inevitably spring up when this is projected into existence. Hence he is no partisan, even when he sees that certain things are in the greater sense right and progressive, others wrong and regressive.

With all this, and an inner quietness, he is far from inactive. He combines the power to observe life with active participation in it. But the participation is not that of the busy seeker after wealth or even the fulfillment of a cause. The source of his action is not the ego, but the spiritual Self, and, as already indicated, he is non-resistive yet can be very positively active at the same time. This form of action is unlike that of our normal habit, where we are really *re*active rather than directly and spontaneously *active*. We do things in response to external stimuli, but the charismatic person originates his activities from a deep inner intuition, and regardless of how it may affect him personally.

He is, moreover, a happy person, in tune with the life around him. He takes things as they are, not as he would like them to be — even if at some moment, this acceptance takes on the form of action to change them because it is necessary to do so. It is not an uproarious happiness, but the serenity one sees on the faces of some of the finest statues of the Buddha — and, unfortunately, on few if any of the figures of the western Christ.

This may suggest that the charismatic person is cold and indifferent. The latter he may be, in the sense that he is unidentified at the psychological level, if only because of his sense of union and identity at the spiritual. Detachment is a very different thing from the ivory tower of isolation which is found in many people. The tower, which is a prison as well as a citadel, means that a wall is put up between oneself and others. The enlightened individual has no such walls, but learns the rightful place of pleasure and pain as a pair on the same level, and accepts both without desire for one or aversion from the other. He is far from insensitive, despite his detachment. On the contrary, it is likely that he is more sensitive than average to all aspects of life, pleasant or unpleasant; but his ego is not caught up in them, so he does not react, even if he experiences deeply.

At the same time, he will have a sense of humor: one without malice or cruelty, never laughing *at* people, but laughing *with* them, and with himself too. For, viewed from the Essential level, it is obvious how ridiculous and childish most human pre-occupations and behavior are, against the deeper realities of life.

This attempt to give a picture of the fully charismatic individual is not merely imaginary. Rather is it synthetic, derived from hints and observations of many people who carry at least something of the quality of Being. If it is at all correct, it would describe one who is near the further end of the road of merely human évolution. Many ordinary people, moreover, become temporarily charismatic, rising to an emergency or a crisis, then falling back again into the general communal level, in much the same way as individuality is seen momentarily among animals. Every human being has this charismatic quality latent in him and capable of being evoked. It is a spiritual quality, and each one of us is, at the roots, spiritual. Beside this, and it is fairly common, a person who is "magnetic," *mana* in the lesser sense, may bring charisma, to a more or less degree, through a biased personality.

In any case, if an individual is ready to receive the charismatic grace, he will do so, even if it comes through an imperfect channel. Here the one who is apparently the recipient is, probably unconsciously, the one through whom the charisma flows, to the benefit of himself and those with whom he is in a living relationship of the kind Buber describes as "I-Thou." He is, as it were, his own priest.

So closely are *mana* and charisma related, moreover, that one-sided *mana* can lead to the charismatic level, while charisma may be distorted and polluted, and become one-sided for good or evil.

We now come to another form of *mana* or charisma which is not so much the possession of an individual as of an office held by that individual. This office has mythical and archetypal value, and is typified by such people as the king or queen of a nation, the head of a religious body.

This matter depends on the relation between individuals which create a collective group. Up to now in the history of man such collectives have inevitably had some idea at their center, and this idea, in an enduring group, has mythical or archetypal roots. This is obvious in a religion such as the Christian, perhaps less so where political, racial or national groups are concerned. Yet the Jewish and Moslem people have a very strong tradition which covers both the political or social and the religious spheres; the Nazi Germans rallied round the old myth of the savage Wagnerian gods; every valley in Norway or Switzerland has its own legends around which myth gathers; and so on, in every part of the world where individuals have formed themselves into a cohesive com-

71

munity.

In other words, every group has its myth, behind which lies its own archetypal principle. It is from this that the power of a nation derives. The religions operate in much the same way, though the boundaries of a religious group often differ from those of a political entity. Islam extends throughout its own world, as do Christianity and Judaism. These archetypal images have something in common throughout mankind, but vary in their emphasis and acquire local coloring besides.

Britain, perhaps, shows us most clearly the combination of the two, the civil and spiritual powers being nominally co-extensive throughout the land, so that the offices of Sovereign and Highpriest are in close relationship, the former though lay, being the technical head of the Anglican Church.

In a collective structure, there are always positions of authority with archetypal significance. The Sovereign represents the active, external power which keeps order in the body politic. The chief priest, the Archbishop of Canterbury, represents the inner authority of spiritual aspiration; and in Britain, this rank is conferred on him and on the next level under him, the "Lords Spiritual", by the same person who is the head of the outer State. (The Archbishop of Canterbury is reckoned while in office to be next after the royal dukes in order of precedence; he is "first peer of the realm.")

There is about royalty an ancient tradition that "the king can do no wrong," that his whimsical requests are commands which must be obeyed, that he has healing power by the touch of his hand. Some of this has become outmoded, but it still remains even among intelligent people, sometimes even in those who think the monarchy an anachronism. It shows not only in ordinary loyalty to the person of the Sovereign, but in the manner in which people flock to Buckingham Palace at times of national crisis or rejoicing, in how people feel comfort if visited by the ruler when calamity has hit a district; this is seen in endless other ways. A bishop or priest, too, is thought to be able to bless or curse, or intervene with God more effectively than a layman, and for the same reason. Both priest and ruler are linked with myth and symbol along a line which has existed from time immemorial; that is, they are part of the perennial philosophy of man. Even where

72

a monarch is tightly bound by a constitution, he derives power both from the fact that he is of the blood royal, and from the fact that by popular assent, he is crowned, anointed, surrounded with ancient symbolism and pageantry. These things are much more meaningful than mere theatricalism or dead custom, by virtue of their archetypal quality: they are realities even in the midst of a materialistic civilization, and of value in that they keep people in touch with their own national archetypes.

Looked at in terms of the individual human being, the king or queen stands for authority, the true will, the power which disciplines the more passional and disorderly nature. The priest, often represented more as an old sage, is his enlightened mind.

In the group, these figures and many others are externalized, and their power is seen as flowing from them by virtue of their symbolic office, not because of what they may be as individual human beings. That this is unconsciously realized is shown in the fact that the Archbishop is a high-ranking peer only while he is in office: when he leaves it, he may still command respect because of his personal qualities, but he is no longer what he was while incarnating an archetypal figure. The same applies to the obscurity which surrounds a deposed or abdicated king.

There is an extension of this matter, too, in that the charismatic power of sovereign and high-priest devolves through the hierarchy of those who serve under them, operating in their name. A police constable, acting "In the name of the Queen" automatically calls out a different response from a mere civilian; the vicar of a country parish is in a position different from that of a member of his congregation, by virtue of his link with the archetypal superior. In the same way, a royal charter gives a university a certain place and authority in the community which a similar institution, not so licensed, would not have.

It is as if the charismatic or *mana* quality in such cases flowed through the office, which in turn, is part of the myth-drama which is at the heart of every nation or religion. And, besides, one is apt to find that certain professions carry with them still the remnants of a *mana* which may long since have become obsolete. The legal profession shows this in the respect expected toward the judiciary, representing indirectly the sovereign on the seat of judgment. The medical profession is still, if only in its own estimation, a priesthood which, even though it may deny any connection with religion, nevertheless speaks of the non-qualified as "laymen."

Thus we have a complex series of problems and layers of what is known generally as *mana*: that which belongs to the individual in his own right; that which belongs to the office which the individual fills, if only temporarily; that which is spiritual or charismatic; and that which is personal, "magnetic" and biased on one side of a pair of complementary expressions of a single basic archetype. The relation of this to expressed myth is also a matter of great interest both as regards a collective group and in the responses of individuals to the principles involved. But basically, the charismatic quality is the same whether flowing through an individual or an office holder or whether it is found in a truly holy place, or around a certain material object which serves as its focus. Those who learn to study themselves as the embodiments of a personal myth eventually touch the charismatic level. That myth displays not only their individual and unique life-pattern, it will also indicate how that pattern is integrated into the wider myth of the culture to which they belong; hence, their link with the collective mind of the group and sub-groups in which they live. Such a one will find reflected in his dreams and visions much that is of immense value to him as he considers them consciously and intelligently. As he discovers himself, the charismatic quality will automatically flow in and through his personality and, properly directed, will be conveyed to those around him as well.

PART II

SPECULATIONS ON THE NEW MIND

We have, so far, endeavored to formulate certain admittedly difficult principles which are at the root of the major change taking place in the collective mind. ·The pattern of that mind is far from clear: it is only at its beginning, and the full development of it will probably be as different from what we already know, as a newborn baby is from its appearance as a foetus. But, like the foetus, its ground plan is already laid down, so that speculation as to its future becomes to some extent permissible on the basis of what we already know.

We have two things to guide us: one, the reports resulting from peak experiences, which show a certain consistency; the other, to consider certain trends felt, and to some extent already revealed in the contemporary world. Using these we can build a model similar to that chemists use in trying to understand the structure of a molecule. If the molecule behaves in a way which does not agree with the model, the latter can be changed to fit in with the new developments until, ultimately, the correct shape is found. So with our suggested pictures.

The basis of the following chapters is that Essential mind is unitary, universal, and so, immortal when viewed from the space-time realm we normally live in. It functions from within outward, or, if we prefer, from above downward, from the Spiritual to the material. The ordinary mind is dual, operates "horizontally" at its own level, though it has a teleological impulsion also to move from the more material toward the more Essential, a tendency which grows as evolution proceeds, and especially when, as now, a major change of balance occurs. The old mind is an outgrowth from instinctive levels. The personal ego develops in it. The new mind, while it includes the old, becomes increasingly influenced from the Spiritual or Numinous level. Hence the values which it demands are very different from the old, being more and more projected into the elaborate existential world from the simplicity of the archetypal realm. The conflicts of the day may be seen to derive from the demands of the new consciousness working against the resistance, the "entropic" tendencies, of the old.

In writing what follows, we are not making prophecies. But in thinking of what seems likely to be our future as a race, one may begin to do something constructive. The very fact that one is endeavoring to understand things seems to have a certain value even now. However distressing some of these things may seem, nevertheless they need to be considered in terms of their possible outcome in a future perhaps not too far remote.

CHAPTER XII

SELF-EXPRESSION

The demand for the right to express oneself, to "be oneself," is perhaps more consciously widespread today than it has ever been. The young person wriggling, alone or in front of a partner, to "pop" music, or taking part in an amorphous "happening" is endeavoring to realize what he or she is. He wants to be free from all the inhibitions of convention, codes of manners and sometimes even of ordinary honesty. Older people may, with reason, be distressed by what is going on; but unless one sees from a wider point of view what it is all about, there is nothing which can effectively be done except possibly to aggravate the manifestations of what is basically a legitimate and natural urge.

The reason behind this outburst of undirected individualism is not far to seek. It is a breakaway from the self-seeking which hitherto has aimed at certain values now tending to be outgrown, such as money, power and prestige, without finding a more positive goal. For Self, ever since it appeared in man as the personal ego, has always sought to expand and express itself. Nature intended it to do so. As self-identity becomes stronger in the course of evolutionary time, this urge naturally grows with it; but in seeking freedom, it encounters obstacles. The first is that of herd morality, that of the super-ego discussed in a previous chapter. This exists not only in the form of social pressure, it manifests also as a subjective, inner factor in each individual. But it is not the only obstacle, or seeming obstacle. The other is teleological, and demands that the Self as reflected at the level of the ego should change in the direction of essential Selfhood. This too is an evolutionary phenomenon.

We see something of the same in the larger context of collective mankind. Groups of all sizes and qualities also seek their identity and meet with resistance which varies from clan to clan, nation to nation, race to race. If frustration becomes too strong, wars break out. As a result there is a more or less successful change of pattern between the groups and also, through their direct influence, on the single individuals involved, who themselves are affected, for better or worse.

It is these individuals who make the group, their aggregate quality being that of the group, which is the sum of them all, with something added which one might call the soul of that aggregate. It makes the group more powerful than it would be if it were merely a collection of discrete men and women. We need at this stage to grasp that each individual is deeply interlocked with the collectivity in which he is born and in which he lives. The group affects him, he affects the group, in a two-way interchange, though the main flow is first in one direction and at a latter evolutionary stage in the other.

The weak individuality of primitive man is at a stage when the mass predominates and determines attitudes and behavior. There is little conflict between the tribe and the tribesman. The infantile ego is carried on the ebb and flow of instinctive collective life, and is largely identified with it. It lives much less by thought than by feeling, the function of which is to merge things together, reaching out, as it were, from individual to individual or from an individual toward an object, and "touching" it. Living beings therefore tend, through feeling, to become identified with one another and with their environment.

It is only as thought becomes active and dynamic that the tendency to separate becomes manifest. The function of thinking is toward objectivity, that is, toward separation between subject and object, hence between ego and what is felt to be non-ego. In this way the mind of the individual begins to acquire a distinctive shape, growing out of the mass. The thinker, if he can eliminate feeling, becomes discrete and really himself. This is what the scientist attempts to do when he sets up experiments, the results of which present facts which cannot be distorted by "wishful thinking," that is by thought animated by feeling. He may succeed in this to some extent, but the scientist with insight realizes that it occurs only within the limited field of his physical or mental laboratory, outside of which he is as much carried by feeling as is any ordinary intelligent human being. Yet if his insight carries him that far, he sees how pleased or disappointed he is if results of experiments tell him what he wants to be true, or else upset his preconceptions.

Self can thus be extricated from the mass by the action of clear, objective thought. But few people, even in these days of scientific and technological training, ever reach or even attempt to reach this point in any part of their daily lives. It is obvious that feeling, acting automatically, below the level of consciousness, is vastly influential in everyday affairs. If it were not so, things like diplomacy, statesmanship, tact, timing of events, would be irrelevant when facts have to be faced. We know only too well how things can go wrong if these lubricants are not in constant use. In the same way, the search for self-expression remains for the majority largely at the level of feeling, below even that of intellectual and scientific thinking.

At that level, as we have suggested, two complementary instinctive forces, that of social morality and that of instinct or libido assail the ego from opposite directions even if the aim of both is the same: security and integrity of the ego. The one urges freedom from trammels, the other, from social pressure. The rules of "the Establishment" the conservative element — using the word in a non-political sense — play into the pattern in opposition to the demand for freedom of the individual. The two are therefore in conflict. For a long time in human development the social factor won the struggle. In Victorian times, it reached its peak, the pattern having changed from morality imposed by physical means such as force of arms, the horrors of the Inquisition and the like, in favor of ostracism and opprobrium for the one outside the pale, making him, often, feel guilty without real cause.

Then came the first world cataclysm, in 1914, when external amenity and morality were set aside on a large scale. In 1919, a form of peace returned, and with it a new order of society. In this, the clash between the two impulses showed itself in the grouping into one category of the younger people of the "twenties," who challenged the accepted order of things. On the other hand there were those who, having had a taste of chaos and disorder in battle, were only too glad to sink back into what they thought would be an orderly existence, running in well oiled grooves. The second, and greater war, widened still further the slightly opened door and so helped the younger generation once more to rebel.

These younger people were, at first, those who had been affected by the war. But now the majority of the rebels are among those who were born after the armed conflict had stopped, and among them one sees a curious phenomenon. For though perhaps the majority are much as they have always been, ordinary, mediocre people, there is a big admixture of others of a new and different type, not seen in large numbers before. One group of these is quite amoral, has no sense of right and wrong and uses violence even where violence is unnecessary, to gain immediate selfish ends. The others, on the other hand, are perhaps rebels and anti-social in their behavior, but they have a maturity and wisdom which goes far beyond that of their elders, even if their practical aims seem wrong.

This latter group are the philosophically minded members of the "anarchists" or "underground." They know what they want even if, for the present, they do not seem able to achieve it, because, they say, the Establishment has too firm a hold on money, politics, economics and agents of law and order such as the police and militia. They frankly say that they want to bring about a new social order where each person will be free. In itself, this is a very desirable thing, except that the human being, let loose in the world, will soon cut across the freedom of others, and so the whole system of law and law enforcement would have to begin all over again. The Marxist man does not exist in fact, any more than the "beautiful people," as they call themselves, are beautiful. Nor are the Utopians real, those who imagine an ideal country populated by their own fantasies. Real people are still on Pope's "isthmus" or Nietzsche's "tightrope."

To understand the seeming chaos of the day, where everything which holds society together seems to be breaking down, we need to seek parallels in the wider evolutionary pattern. These can be seen at the biological level where seed is apparently destroyed to produce a plant, blossom decays into fruit, and so on. The ovum breaks down to liberate the larva, the larva "dies" into the pupa, the pupa turns into the imago. The vertebrate embryo grows within the amnion, but, if it is to live, eventually bursts out of it. In all cases, something is destroyed that something new may live.

It is the same in human society, where evolutionary trends show mainly at the mental level. We are witnessing today the breakdown of the old mold and the emergence of a new order though, like the new-born of any species, it is still unstable, unlicked, perhaps even rather ugly. Ideologies, creeds, institutions, are the mental equivalents of the membranes or husks around any germinating entity. Having served their purpose, these must of necessity be discarded. But collective humanity cannot exist without some containing form, a fact that many of the thoughtful rebels realize. They do not want anarchy in the sense of complete lack of government or law; but they demand a brand new order, where there will be more self-determination and therefore freedom even to do foolish things, provided they do not upset other people. That their idea of how this can happen is often fantastic and quite incapable of realization does not mean that the impulse is anything but progressive.

The trouble is that the resistance the new movement meets at the hands of the more conservative moralists forces it into a personal, "horizontal" struggle where the individual at the ego level of selfhood is at war with the social, tribal dictates operating at the same level. The healthy evolutionary trend however is "vertical," from the personal, existential level toward the Essential, and hence, would operate from a new type of consciousness, a new level of the mind.

From another angle, the new life impulse is the masculine, dynamic element capable of fertilizing the feminine, preservative aspect of existence. Both are equally necessary in all growing systems, physical or mental. In the present war between the two, the dynamic side is the stronger, whence disintegration predominates over construction: we have, to use an old tag, "revolution rather than evolution". From the level of Essence or Tao, the need is to find cooperation between the two. To channel a stream is to add to its strength, and to guide it in the right direction. To dam it up is to court disaster. Yet in both cases, the water is the same. Similarly, many explosive substances can be burned harmlessly in open vessels, whereas, imprisoned, let us say in a gun barrel or a shell-casing, they explode destructively.

The balance needed cannot be found easily. Least of all does it exist when the main tension is between two generations differing not only in physical age but, often, in their mental make-up. Yet both have a contribution to make toward an integrated and balanced society.

This, however, cannot be brought about by individuals who are themselves at odds within themselves, as many people are today, especially the young. Ultimately, the solution comes from the individual man. Some part of him wants freedom to express himself, another part is afraid of this and of the isolation which seems to come with individualism. This arises from the sense of self-identity of the ego at the personal, instinctive level. As we have tried to indicate, the one who knows Selfhood at a point nearer to the Essential, loses that fear because what seems irreconcilable to the personal mind merges with its opposite as it gets nearer the archetypal, essential plane of Being.

How can this confusion be resolved? First by realizing that we are confused. We are not clear as to what are real values, what is the meaning of life. Our arts and literature today continually harp on this theme and, when the creative artist fails to find the answer, the result is the nihilism and squalor of such writers as the older generation of the French existentialists, the "existential vacuum" as it has been called.

These writers, however, indirectly suggest the solution. For had they not somewhere in themselves a feeling of something beyond, they would not become so deeply depressed. But this "something" is a challenge to present attitudes, to present mental habits, which they are unwilling to accept, and so repress into the unconscious realm. When such people surrender to their inner knowledge, the whole picture changes, and existence takes its place as an aspect of deeper Being. The surrender, however, involves giving up escapes and evasions, whether doctrinal or through drugs or the cult of purely animal pleasures; for these are seen, not as self-expression but as betrayals of Self-expression. In contrast to this, the expression of essential Selfhood brings with it the archetypal aspect of things, and this is the factor which makes any creative act real: the reality of the true as against meretricious ideologies, religions, or art.

Chapter XIII

PERCEPTION AND PERCEPTIVITY

It may at first sight appear that these two words refer to the same thing. Their common root is *per,* through, and *capio,* I seize or understand. But when we say colloquially that a person is deeply perceptive, we mean something more than his ability to use his senses in the act of perception. Hence it will be well to recognize that there are two ways by which we learn to know the world in which we live.

Perception is, by definition, the use of the physical senses as a means of cognition of the objects around us. Impulses strike the sense organs, whence they are relayed to the brain, where they are in some measure translated and classified. After this they become *percepts* in the center of consciousness. The simple percept is then further worked upon by association, memory, sense of similarity or difference, in which other percepts are brought together and the result is meaningful *apperception,* a stage further than simple perception. This means that the perceptive act, triggered off by impulses from the outer world, takes place in the computer-like mechanism of the mind. Apperception represents a building up and synthesizing of the simpler elements into a higher order of ideation which results from the repetition of similar events. This is what we call experience. So the individual grows.

Perception, however, is usually thought of as only an incoming process. Light strikes the retina, and the rest follows more or less successfully. But to experience what a light-pattern means implies that the mind has, as it were, invisibly to project something out from itself in order to make contact with the object from which the light rays are reflected. We often say, "My eye followed . . ." an object, "My attention was caught by . . ." whatever it is. This suggests that meaningful perception is in reality a two-way operation between subject and object, making a field between them, as between two poles, and that it is in this polar field that understanding may arise. The origin of the process, however, is the object, not the mind.

Perceptivity means much more than this, and operates from a point within the mind itself. Perception takes place at the level of the discursive or existential mind, but perceptivity starts at the Essential level, where there is awareness of complete unity between what, at a lower level, would be Self and not-self. Such sense of unity is achieved because nothing interposes between the two; there is, as one man expressed it, "a perfect interface" between them. No memory, association, feeling of like or dislike intervenes, no discursive thinking about the object. If the individual can experience such a thing in its complete nakedness, he has full understanding of the apparent object of his study, he realizes his oneness with that object. This unimpaired vision is at the summit of spiritual consciousness. It is out of time, complete, still; and it is blissful. Moreover, it is beyond being questioned. The individual is certain of the truth of what he has seen, yet in a paradoxical way, he remains flexible in mind, so that he is neither cocksure, dogmatic, nor fanatical at the personal level. Jung was once asked whether he believed in God. He felt able to reply, "I do not believe, *I know.*" And one can assume that he said this quietly and without undue emphasis, and moreover that his God would not be the anthropomorphic god of most people.

Perception is, clearly, dependent on there being certain open channels into the mind. It is a faculty which can be trained and developed by repeated experiences. An expert mechanic often knows that something is wrong with a machine long before this is obvious to the untrained layman. A painter acquires a fine sense of color values, but he may be tone deaf to music. Both of these people *perceive* but neither is necessarily *perceptive* in the inward sense of that word.

On the other hand, a great artist like Beethoven could not have written his finest works without a high degree of true perceptivity; and he was able to go on composing long after his physical perception of sound had broken down. Doubtless he was helped by his previous experience, but perceptivity still operated and he was still deeply creative in a manner which showed his touch with the Essential, Archetypal world.

In its essence, perceptivity is an overall sensibility of the mind itself, regardless of any sensory channels or means of expressing by direct means what that perceptivity reveals. There are many more perceptive artists than there are those who are able to project themselves into creative works. But the dumb, receptive seer cannot but be influenced by his visions so that his life becomes in some way an expression of his sensibility. Edward Carpenter, a largely forgotten philosopher today, expressed this when he said in *Angels' Wings* that if a person listened to a great symphony and was not in some way changed in his attitude to life, he had not heard the symphony.

In principle, then, perceptivity brings one into knowledge of things archetypal, spiritual, numinous. It opens out increasingly if, by whatever means, a person raises his mental consciousness away from that of the instinctual, mundane level of material life. It is the quality of mind which is needed if we are, collectively, to bring about a new world order based on truer values than those of material benefit.

It will be noted that we have, so far, not brought into our picture any mention of extra-sensory perception (ESP) or "psychism." This has been, as in earlier discussion, in order to emphasize in principle the different modes by which we learn to know our context in the universe. Perception operates, as we have said, in the polarity between "I" and "Not I"; perceptivity is from the unity of "We," which can also be expressed as "I-thou," showing a living relationship quite other than "I-him/her/it."

ESP is in reality just what it says: perception extended into a region where the physical senses no longer operate. If this definition is accepted, it applies as much to the telescopes and other instruments we use, as to "psychic" powers. The instruments are an outward extension of the senses, the "psychic" functions of clairvoyance and the rest are their subjective counterparts. *Both have their origin at the level of physical sensation.* Many people today are interested in ESP because it opens up a field which is wider than that of the physical world, the invisible one of our first chapter. In this way it is a step toward numinous enlightenment; but if we consider it in the light of what we have said above, it is very far from being illumined vision. It is surprising how even highly intelligent people will say to a person reputedly clairvoyant or able to use some other form of ESP with a degree of control, "You are psychic, therefore you *know*." They then proceed to ask for information of a most recondite order, or sometimes about purely material facts that it would be impossible to give. Moreover, they will lose all sense of judgment and accept as true the most extravagant statements of mediums and people who claim to receive messages from the highest spiritual entities, or from people in outer space; and that, without considering for a moment whether these messages make even ordinary sense. If we go into the matter, we shall find that, whereas ESP touches a field supplementary to that of the senses, hence, widens the total range of perception of an individual, it is limited by the very same factors as inevitably limit the operations of the ordinary discursive mind.

ESP, then, is an extension of sensation. It will be useful now to fill in a gap which exists between ESP proper and the ordinary physical range. This has been recently called Metasensory Perception and the term is useful in connection with certain phenomena.

It has been found that some individuals respond to stimuli, usually auditory, under circumstances when by the ordinary laws of physics they should not do so. Two astronomers in the Sierra Nevada of California caught sight of a very bright fire-ball or meteorite crossing the sky. One commented on the rushing noise which went with it, the other heard nothing. Similar instances were recorded on other occasions, sometimes when careful observation of the location of the meteor was possible. They seemed to occur in an area where local electro-magnetic disturbances took place during the phenomena, but too far away for airborne sound to have been heard until some time afterward. These cases were the subject of a paper published by the Rand Corporation of America* and were supplemented in a newspaper report where it was said that an engineer working with a team discovered that he heard a buzzing sound whenever a radar station was in action. Experi-

*"Anomalous Sounds & Electromagnetic Effects Associated with Fireball Entry" — Mary F. Rorig and Donald L. Laman. Memo RM 3724 ARPA, July 1963

ments showed (a) that the sound could be shut off when the man was screened with wire gauze, (b) that when a hole was cut in this and put over his ear, he still heard nothing; but (c) that if the hole were placed somewhere over the parietal or temporal region of the skull, he heard it clearly but, obviously, through some center in the brain other than that connected with the ears. In England, while the V2 rockets were falling, a good number of people found themselves giving a nervous start ten or fifteen seconds before the actual sound of the shock wave and the explosion reached them through the air.

All these things suggest that there are centers of perception which respond to a range beyond those of the ordinary senses (hearing, at least) and which record physical stimuli at a level beyond that of dense physical vibration. But they are not in the more remote field of true extrasensory perception which includes clairvoyance, precognition, telepathy and the rest. We are, however, able to postulate that perception extends along a range from physical sensation to true extrasensation of non-physical events, with metasensory perception linking the physical and the non-physical. But all of these operate within the field of the discursive levels of the mind.

Essential perceptivity, however, works from the other pole, and hence in the opposite direction from perception. It starts in the archetypal world, and comes "down" or "out" from this into the existential world, where it may be said to meet the sensory and extra-sensory range in its upper levels. True perceptivity shows us things *as they are*. Perception shows them to us colored by our personal minds and, like Shelley's "dome of many-colored glass," "stains the white radiance" of the archetypal reality. Perceptivity is outside the realm of *maya,* of the pairs of opposites, of distortion, while perception belongs to that realm and is only relatively true in what it presents to us.

In practice, it is evident that complete perceptivity belongs only to the perfected man whereas, we "in the middle state," at best mingle the two. What truth there is in perception may be said to be due to an infusion into it of perceptivity or illumination, whereas the expression of true perceptivity becomes distorted and conditioned by the language of ordinary perception.

This mingling is the cause of much confusion when people

begin to study the less earthy and well explained forms of perception. They fail to realize that even the finest form of ESP does not of necessity involve archetypal perceptivity. Our semantic habits have not reached the point where the two factors, and the expression of their findings, can be distinguished. The same language has to be used for both, even though the act of cognition is in each case quite different, the one originating in the realm of Truth, the other in that of relativity or *maya;* the first, by definition, incapable of being anything but accurate, the other equally of necessity being relatively tinted and distorted.

The distinction, moreover, shows us the validity of the Raja Yoga admonition to the student that he should not try to develop psychic powers *(siddhis)* but strive only after direct enlightenment after which the lesser range of perception, including ESP, will develop at the right time and in the right way. If he tries to force matters by "sitting for development," by the use of drugs or Tantric or Hatha Yoga exercises, hypnosis or other means, the result can only be frustration of the larger vision which is the goal of all true yoga, by whatever name it is called. It tells us too that an individual may be deeply perceptive yet show no signs of clairvoyance, clairaudience or other of the modalities of ESP along the lines of the physical senses. He may, however, express his inner vision in his way of life, or through the forms of real art, more accurately than he could if he were to try to translate it directly into sensory language. On the other hand, it sometimes happens that this perceptivity is able to find direct expression along the track of one or other of the physical senses. An individual who is deeply sensitive to form or color may thus be one of the rare accurate clairvoyants, another perhaps a musician, clairaudient, another, steeped in history finds that he can "psychometrize" (to use an outmoded term) the history of place or object without drawing on phantasy and imagination.

Perception can thus be defined as a reaching-out of the mind toward an object from which sensory (or extra-sensory) stimuli are received. It tends toward *identification,* i.e. creating an identity, between the observer and the object. *Perceptivity,* however, is based on awareness of essential *identity* — something which *is,* and does not have to be *made,* as in identification — and which is experienced by the removal or stilling of what intervenes between the two so that that unity is experienced through Being.

Finally, a word about the much abused term intuition. People often say "I can't trust my intuition; it is so often wrong." The reply is that if it is wrong it is not intuition which is at work but some emotional impulse. By definition, intuition must be right. It consists in making a valid decision beyond that permissible in strictly rationalistic terms. It is often referred to as "feminine" because more women than men accept and live by it. It is actually just as prevalent among the male sex but it is not so easily recognized because it brings in, beside intellectual considerations, feelings which may even over-ride the logical conclusions which intellectual factors point to. Men pride themselves on being logical and rational; they are not so in fact.

Just as we have divided perception from perceptivity, so intuition can be said to operate from two levels. In one case it may or may not include extra-sensory data of which an individual may not even be conscious. It takes into account such imperceptible subtleties of physical sense perception as a change of muscular tension or facial expression, and builds up a synthetic image of a situation which presents itself directly to the mind in giving the meaning and truth about outer situations.

The other form of intuition is the immediate and unextended knowledge arising from the inner, essential unity which shows one an object or a situation as it were from within, and complete. This order of intuition is the first step toward what may or may not become clothed in sensory language. Many people, and especially the more sensitive, artistic, religious persons, are thus deeply intuitive, and know the reality of a situation. The clinical sense of the good doctor, the understanding of others found in some people; the love, the sense of wonder, of mystery, of the Life in everything; all these spring from the intuitive level which is rooted in true Being and not only in the associative, sensory-perceptive aspects of the ordinary mind. Again, such a state is not achieved by *trying* to become intuitive, but by the achievement of inner numinous qualities. Then, as the Hindus tell us, the *siddhis* or psychic powers, both of perception and action, develop of themselves as a sideline to the quest for Truth.

Chapter XIV

NOW

One of the attitudes which seems to be changing today is our outlook on time. The phrase, "the time-track," has been in use for some while, and on that track we recognize past, present and future as the three phases of time. Past and future have been considered as the main factors extending indefinitely in either direction from an evanescent present which is an almost fictional junction and division between the two really important dimensions. But under the influence of the newly developing mind, another attitude is growing. This stresses the present, the *now*, in such a way as to make us feel that this is of far more interest both in creation and in perceptivity than either past or future. Indeed, existentialism as a cult, focuses around immediate experience, seeking a full appreciation of it as it occurs, then letting it go into the past, to be replaced by a series of new "existential moments."

When one considers the matter, it is not difficult to see that the present is the only place in time from which the ordinary mind consciously operates. As it looks back on the past and tries to see the future, the mind actually stands where these two meet, and uses this point in order to make its assessment of both. Indeed, those people are right who tell us that *the historian* creates history. History is not the actual events which have occurred but his view of them. He uses events as material with which to build up the scene he shows us, but he does so in the present. He evaluates the past by hindsight which, however accurate, is nevertheless not at all the same as actually dwelling in past centuries as a contemporary. Similarly, foresight, even commonsense planning, is done from the present moment. The envisaged future, moreover, often contains a reflection of the past, over the hinge of the present: what has happened already is likely to happen again unless we *now* introduce new factors to deflect that repetition. These factors are basically produced by a movement in our own mentality. If our minds remain closed to anything new, the future we create must, obviously, resemble the past we should now be leaving behind. Ouspensky, indeed, goes so far as to suggest that events repeat themselves exactly, in a closed circle, unless new forces are brought into play. This cannot be true, if only because through the flow of universal or cosmic time, the old "now" is replaced by a succession of new ones; apart from astronomical changes, this means that nothing is exactly where it has been, even in human life.

This is the usual pattern of time in our minds. But as contact with numinous and archetypal images increases, one sees that this is not the whole picture. It is valid enough for the existential mind. But if we take into account some less commonplace factors, we find that it can happen, and indeed, does so much more frequently than a casual glance may show, that the mind upsets the natural flow of time through itself. It does this either by retrocognition of a past for which there are as yet no historical data, or by precognizing or prophesying events which have not yet happened but which will do so. J. W. Dunne's old book, *An Experiment with Time*, the literature of psychical research, and indeed the experiences of some who have used psychedelic drugs, give many examples of both.

These experiences suggest that, while physical time is cogged into the mechanism of the material universe, there is also a level where, as we have argued, time ceases to exist, and eternity, measureless and boundless is known. Between the two there lies what Jung in a private letter called psychic time, describing it as plastic and flexible. It is not rigid as physical time is, but, since mental or psychic events are sequential, it is not timeless. It is the kind of time we know in dreams, where many events may seem to crowd into a very brief instant of clock time, or the reverse.

Such an idea would account for the strange phenomenon of precognition: for how on earth (using this phrase both literally and colloquially) can one see accurately something which has not yet happened? It cannot happen "on earth" but in the mental realm it appears as if time could in some way be warped, put out of line, so that the present moment is temporarily displaced into the future. Then it returns to the clock-time present, bringing with it what it has seen in another "now" equally valid.

These freaks of experience (and, as Dunne suggests, they are really constantly occurring though we do not pay attention to them) are relevant to the theme that the timeless is, in its own way, directly linked through the mind with the present instant of our consciousness in the physical world. Normally, being unbounded at its own level, the present contains past and future within itself. At the physical level it may be said to spread backward and forward from the immediate moment.

Briefly, the conclusion is that time is cyclic, polarized, fully existential. In the Numinous world it is not polarized into past and future, it is replaced by a "Now" which forever IS. In the intermediate, mental levels, rigid natural or clock time mingles with the timeless, so that, while there is still a sequential order, this is not found to be a rigid frame of reference.

As far as man is concerned, the chain linking the numinous, timeless world with the physical plane runs through the mental or psychic field, to impinge on the physical realm at the present moment. In other words, *the physical present is a direct reflection of the Eternal*. But in practice this projection of eternity becomes involved in the mental realm and so loses its directness. It is as if a ray of white light passed through lenses, prisms, opacities, before reaching the screen which is its goal. So the immediacy of impact of the Spiritual world on the material is distorted, except, so far, at peak moments.

Once more we are faced with the illusion, or *maya*-producing, qualities of the instinctive, personal mind. But the germ of the new order of mentality evokes a fire-like quality which, while it may destroy, is also a purifier and a rectifier of distortions. Intuitively, moreover, we feel that by operating from the material end, this new force is capable, as we learn how, of clearing the mental field so that the transcendental and the archetypal show us the meaning of life while we are still in our physical, waking consciousness.

This, in other language, seems to be what Tillich meant when he spoke of the need to be concerned with real Ultimates and Absolutes, and not to be deflected into giving absolute value to the less-than-ultimate. *Now*, in physical consciousness, is an absolute in that, if it can be freed from the clutter of past or future, it directly reflects the Noumenon. The relation between the two is another aspect of the Jacob's ladder of an earlier chapter. But it also suggests that there is no intrinsic need to climb that ladder through expressed myth, religious disciplines, yoga, and the rest. The top can be reached by a form of direct spiritual insight. Disciplines and practices may be useful, for a time. But they are not (as we have said) essential, and indeed at some stage, may become an obstacle when we begin to see the all-powerful forces behind the concept of the "Now."

This way of putting things is far from new. It is being put forward today principally by Krishnamurti, and by others. It is also to be found in the ancient Tibetan *Book of the Dead* or *Bardö Thödol.* Here it is said that at the moment of physical death, or very soon after, the properly prepared individual soul has a chance of becoming free from the Wheel which takes him into birth after birth and death after death. If he is inwardly ready, there is an instant in which the whole of his past and of his future lie before him. *If he is mentally and emotionally detached from them,* he can, at that instant, move away as it were in another dimension, and enter Nirvana. It is worth noting that many people who have come to the very edge of death, especially from drowning, report on the retrospective vision of their whole life. They do not speak of the glimpse of the future, but this may be due to the fact that they did not actually die, so had only half of the whole experience. One can only speculate about this. Hand in hand with it there is the strange idea which has come into Christianity, that the moment a person dies, even full of bad qualities, he can, by a moment of recantation however brief, become "one of God's saints" and be gathered up into permanent heaven. This seems to be an intuition of what might happen as an immediate consummation, perhaps unlikely, for the ordinary "sinner." Most people, according to the Tibetan doctrine, are likely to be still mentally and emotionally tied, and so miss the moment, and at once start on a further round of birth and death.

Today we realize that, while death — and perhaps some moment before birth — may be a time of special opportunity, it is at least theoretically possible for a man to become liberated at any instant of peak experience when the deeper Numen shines through into his physical consciousness. Such moments, however, are usually only partial, only a rift through mental clouds, not a vision of clear sky. The full vision, the one which would bring about Liberation, Enlightenment, *moksha,* Salvation in the true sense, must be like the sun shining in a cloudless sky; that is, where the mind is entirely clear and translucid and there is no unconcious left.

Our minds are, however, as yet anything but clear. Perhaps, by a curious juxtaposition of ideas, we feel that such clarity lies in the future, after much time and work. From the point of view of the new mentality, however, it may be seen otherwise. To think in terms of the future, to see the goal a long way off, is one of the illusions in the existential mind. In reality, the transformation of our ordinary selves into that of the liberated man could take place Here and Now, at any instant. What demands time is the preparation of the mind in such a way that it becomes sufficiently free and buoyant to be ready for the immediate moment of take-off from the material level into the empyrean of Essence. We are, unfortunately, usually taught to think in terms of endless disciplines and practices so that, at some future date, we may find ourselves reaching the consummation we are seeking. It is as if an aircraft were to seek its goal at the end of the runway, whereas its real aim is to fly in another dimension. The level run is necessary, but its length is not arbitrarily fixed. So it is with ourselves.

It seems therefore that by tying ourselves down to the idea of enlightenment or liberation in the future, we defeat ourselves. A new attitude would be to see the act of liberation as immediate, utterly simple, effortless, actionless and obvious. Our minds are used, when they seek to do something, to be complicated, strenuous, busy, and to look afar. Were we able to be still, to *allow* Life to flow through us, instead of trying to *live it* actively, to be permissive without even trying to put a name or label to events as they happen, we should probably find ourselves where we want to be "in a moment, in the twinkling of an eye." The task is so simple that we cannot do it, so obvious we cannot see it, so immediately before us that we look past it: hence it seems to us today infinitely difficult and remote. In reality it is not.

We have headed this chapter "Now," and discussed things in terms of time. But time has its twin, space. It needs to be added that all that has been said can, *mutatis mutandis*, be applied to space too. "Now" is coupled with "Here," the dimensionless, sizeless point in space which is nevertheless the center "from which all parts of the circumference are equidistant" — when we reach our balance in it. In these terms, our extended minds are not centered: they are either eccentric in the mathematical sense, or else elliptical,

The ellipse is a very useful analogy to our present state, and can be used to illustrate three main phases in human life. (See diagram.) Geometrically, an ellipse is drawn round two centers or foci separated by a certain distance, but related to one another. If one then draws a circle round each focus, these may or may not overlap. But as the circles grow bigger, or, alternatively, the foci draw nearer together, there appears an area in the form of a *vesica piscis* where the circles intersect. If, little by little, the two foci move together they become the center of a single circle and the ellipse is no longer in any sense eccentric. If the foci are equated with the Self and the ego, the ellipse is the total man, as yet not fulfilled. The circles round these foci are respectively the personality and (inaccurately, since it is without limits) the field of the Self. When the circles overlap, the vesica is the "area" where archetypal images appear; and the single-centered circle is man perfected.

If, further, we think in terms of a space-time continuum, it is obvious that "Now" and "Here" merge into one and are interchangeable concepts only for semantic purposes.

In conclusion, we may allow ourselves to play lightly with some ideas which arise out of our consideration of space-time as "constructs" in our minds. In Reality, the space-time continuum must be something very different from what we think we know. Our lives are built round a certain picture of this continuum which is general to mankind on this earth. Time flows, space is three-dimensionally fixed, despite the modifications brought to our thought by Einstein.

Suppose, however, that our minds were so structured that we changed things, allowing space to flow through fixed time instead of the reverse. This would give us a very different picture of universal

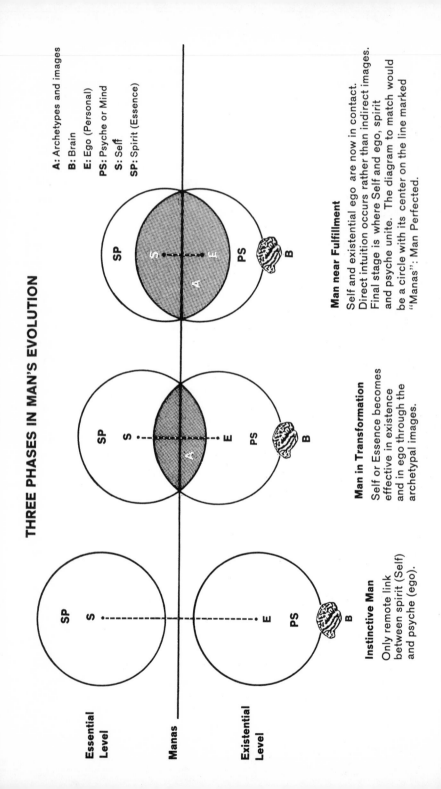

THREE PHASES IN MAN'S EVOLUTION

A: Archetypes and images
B: Brain
E: Ego (Personal)
PS: Psyche or Mind
S: Self
SP: Spirit (Essence)

Essential
Level

Manas

Existential
Level

Instinctive Man

Only remote link
between spirit (Self)
and psyche (ego).

Man in Transformation

Self or Essence becomes
effective in existence
and in ego through the
archetypal images.

Man near Fulfillment

Self and existential ego are now in contact.
Direct intuition occurs rather than indirect images.
Final stage is where Self and ego, spirit
and psyche unite. The diagram to match would
be a circle with its center on the line marked
"Manas": Man Perfected.

facts; one we cannot possibly conceive. Even if one of the three dimensions of space became fluid as time froze, there would be a revolution in our apprehension of things.

This in turn allows us to speculate that, if there are on other planets, the evolutionary equivalent of man on this one, whether or not they had bodies similar to ours (which is dubious for many reasons) their minds might be of such a nature that they would make no contact with ours at the existential level. Thus we might land on Mars, or Venusians land on earth, and find no trace whatever of what might be a teeming humanity of another type, native to that planet. We might be able even to live and establish our own civilization there, and they on our earth, without either being aware of the other.

This may seem idle speculation and is, of course, quite unproven. But it may do something toward bringing nearer to our minds the universal concept of angels or *devas*, who are said to share the earth with us. They might be such a kingdom of intelligent entities as ourselves, but with no meeting point except that suggested by scriptural writings. That point of "crossing" or coincidence would be in the dimensionless realm we speak of as Numinous, Spiritual or Divine, which is why, traditionally, when man sees an angel, he sees him as a god-like Being bringing him a "message" from on High. In other words, the beholder is himself in an exalted state of consciousness in touch with the realm of Being. So he realizes a contact with another dimension of life and intelligence which is not his own human one.

Chapter XV

GOD AND MYSELF

If the principle of *yin-yang* polarity, "reconciled" by Tao, is firmly grasped, it will pursue us everywhere and is a means of dealing with all aspects of life. We shall, again and again, forget it, become confused as between the right and wrong of a situation; but the mental act of returning to this principle will sooner or later help us to make our decision how to act or what attitude to take. We are enmeshed in *maya,* ignorance, at best incomplete understanding. In Christian terminology, we are "estranged" from our true nature, God. Our whole quest, when we have become even slightly aware of this, and of how befogged we are, is to seek for God, Essence, Being, Tao, and to have done with Pope's "middle state."

The quest is Religion in the truest sense. It does not matter whether we pursue our search in churches or temples, schools of teaching, through science or art, through action or in the quietness of our own hearts. These are merely ways of seeking, useful disciplines or techniques for freeing our minds to the point where we can go on without them. For, basically, the Way is both unique for each of us, and can only be trodden alone and unsupported except from within. Indeed, we ourselves *are* that Way, as well as its Goal. It is our Self in the deepest sense in which that word can be understood; we *are* immanent God, Christ, Spirit, and the goal is with us here, now, always and everywhere; but we do not know this because we are so much concerned with existence that we constantly turn our backs on Reality. In Plato's myth, our minds concentrate on the shadows cast on the wall of the cave — the "cave of the heart" — not realizing that they are shadows, *mayavic* figures, and, further, that *they are thrown by Reality itself*. We need only turn around to see It, and realize our own self-deception.

At the same time, the very fact that we can separate the concept of Reality from that of the unreal is important. It derives from the duality of the workaday mind. From the Essential viewpoint, as Professor Ernest Wood has pointed out, *maya* or illusion itself is comprised within total Reality. The totality of *maya* is Reality. It is, however, for us to try to understand both the function of *maya* in that Reality, and what is its purpose and value in the awakening of the human mind and in furthering its movement toward ultimate enlightenment.

It seems that without becoming "estranged," enmeshed in the unreal, mankind would not make any progress. It would remain sterile, blind, asleep, unconscious: it would be the Prodigal's stay-at-home brother, of no account in the universal scheme. This "unreality," made apparent by means of the *yin-yang* polarization becomes increasingly important to us as we seek to approach the basic Unity we call by the name of God or by any other name. For, as we have indicated, whereas we can go a long way living simply in terms of "either/or," of accepting or siding with one aspect or another of a question, we gradually have to assume a position of "both/and," seeing all sides of any situation, in order to understand it fully.

Our daily lives are full of such situations, perhaps the most constant and obvious of which is physical sexual difference. For it seems that the greatest divergence between the poles shows itself in physical matters, gradually diminishing as we proceed inward into the mind, and then beyond it to the Essential levels of our Being. But even bodily sex is not complete: every male body contains rudiments of the female organs, and equally every female has traces of the male. Even here there is no absolute division into black and white, there is only at most a black-grey and a grey which is all but white. This is much more the case within the mind. Everyone has both masculine and feminine characteristics in the psyche, and the more awakened individual tends to show these increasingly as he develops. The greatest creative thinkers of the day know that their feminine intuition plays in with their masculine intellect, that feeling and thought combine to give them their deeper insights. In their daily lives, one finds many mathematicians who are deeply musical, many scientists endowed with a profound aesthetic sense, and many artists who are also very practical and logical, combining both feeling and intellect with intelligence.

One can account for this as one wishes. The admixture may be attributed to pure genetics or education, or it may be explained also in terms of long experience through many lives. What matters is that the more enlightened and awake the mind, the less it can be classed as only masculine or feminine.

At the same time, however, it is important for each person to fit into his or her individual life-pattern. One who is in a female body needs, for mental health and balance, to behave like a woman and to allow her feminine mental traits full play, and vice versa. In both cases, the other pole can be increasingly active in the total mentality, but it belongs to the more subjective levels and should not try to force itself to the outer sphere where it conflicts with the physical organism and its instinctual demands. It is perfectly right that a woman should be intellectual and active, provided she is also willing to play a woman's role in the world, and for a man to be sensitive and intuitive without losing his virility and becoming effeminate. The two qualities should be integrated and at the same time operate where, for the time being, they belong. If there is any truth in the principle of cyclic incarnations, the person who is in a man's body in one life may well be a woman in another, so that in the deeper, essential levels of the mind, experience of both the poles accumulates and eventually gives a balance which is hermaphrodite when seen from the view of the totality of any individual.

At the personal level, however, the integrated individual will live and act according to the Tao of the time which has produced for him a body of a particular sex. From an Essential point of view an individual is not a man or a woman. He is a human being occupying a man's or a woman's body.

These things cannot be proved, of course, but they are the intuitive feelings of a good many thoughtful people. To see them clearly, however, they need to be considered against the background of Essence, and also in terms of the cyclic law which governs existence and ordinary living.

The latter applies in what, to some, may seem inconsistent desires and behavior, in changes from one thing to another, either in general life or in particular departments of it. There are, of course, unstable people who never stay anywhere for long, they find dissatisfaction wherever they may be, as soon as enthusiasm wanes; they often, in so doing, evade rather than fulfil themselves. Others follow, even unconsciously, a definite pattern of movement from one thing to another.

In the subject we are now discussing, man's search for essential Truth, it may mean that, for a time, an individual will find his path by conforming to outer forms such as those of a church. Then, later, he may turn inward into himself, finding no need for the outer expression, and indeed possibly finding that his habits, mental and physical, demand a break if he is not to become caught in something which, for a time, will only impede his progress.

A moderately intelligent woman said, in the course of analytical treatment, that she felt that she needed the external discipline and the observances of the Roman Church. They gave shape and support to her daily life. A few years later she said that she had, for the time being at least, broken away, because she felt that she should now walk alone, even if she often fell down and made mistakes. It did not follow, however, that she would forever repudiate her church. She was, in other words, using her inner sense of individual Being from moment to moment, without tying herself either to past associations or to future hopes. Having used a splint for her broken mind, she had now realized that she should do without it and exercise and strengthen it by its own innate powers. But she recognized that there might come another time when she would find external support once more of value. She kept alive in far more than the physical sense, because of her inner resources.

Putting matters in terms of myth, she had discovered at one period of life that she needed to live in acts which expressed the human predicament and its resolution in general, mythical terms expressed in public worship; then she passed on to living subjectively and more individually, substituting her own inner authority for that claimed by her church.

It should be made clear at this point that to "live out one's myth" does not of necessity mean that anybody needs to go through the stages of analyzing dreamed, spoken, or acted dramas which have come down, sometimes through millennia, with their archetypal figures and symbols. The same can be done otherwise, at least after a time, as there develops a sense of direct orientation toward the Pole Star we have called Essence. In practice this means that, having learned perhaps what dreams show about oneself in a general way, there comes a time when this is no longer necessary and they can be allowed to pass without applying to them any explicit interpretation, such as that learned during analysis. One may even go further, and suggest that after a time constant analytical work becomes a drug, a form of idolatry which stands between the individual and inner Reality. This is a thing often found not only among the patients of analytical psychologists but among the analysts themselves. As Jung, the father of his own kind of dream analysis, himself pointed out, the intellectual and conscious study of dream and its relation to external myth is only a first step, tilling the ground. The creative insight occurs only when quiet and silence once more reign, whether within the mind of a person or between him and his analyst.

In one set of terms, what we are now seeking is the Center, God. We feel we have to travel toward Him, to "find" or "come closer to" Him. This, however, seen from another angle, is not true. The developing mind arrives at a stage where things appear quite otherwise, as many mystics and seers testify. We do not have to look for God: he is there all the time, and no movement or travel is needed to find him. All that is required is, as Patanjali, the great yogi teacher, puts it, to stop "the modifications of the thinking principle," in other words, to still the mind. Anybody who has tried to do this, as it were by force of will, knows that it is impossible, so some other technique is needed and, indeed, is probably implied. In more modern terms we might put it that we have to learn to detach ourselves from the busy-ness of the mind and let it go its own way while our atten-

102

tion is focused on That which we are seeking. To do so involves a different view of life from that of the existential mind. The latter sees life as a journey along the time track; the essential mind is concerned with the Here and Now. Our difficulty is to extricate ourselves from the former. Were we able to do this we should find ourselves gathered up in consciousness into the present instant, unextended from it either backward or forward in time, or "elsewhere" in space, and in that moment consciousness and selfhood would, as it were, move off into the realm of pure Being.

This, in theory, is easy enough. But our mental habits persist and we find ourselves remembering the Vision after it has occurred and more or less explicitly wanting it to be renewed. Doing this, or hoping for its future recurrence automatically frustrates. For we are then being dragged away from the immediate, and are no longer fully centered in it. The place in ourselves which, if empty, would have room for a new moment of Vision is filled by our habit of mental association, by desire-filled memory or anticipation. There is no room for God: or if there is, it is only in an exiguous space in a cluttered room, so that whatever god we perceive can only be a personal, conditioned and relative deity — the one who is, of necessity, in opposition to his light-bringing adversary, Satan or Lucifer.

This is why some of the deepest exponents of "the Way" teach that it is only when the personal "I" is defeated, killed, or, better, allowed to die out that we find what we are looking for. Francis Thompson's *The Hound of Heaven* tells us this in poetry; Patanjali puts it in his own language; we have, as already discussed, the same idea in the Christian Passion; in the death of the Hero in so many myths, before he is reborn. The quest is, in a sense, one of becoming entirely permissive, unresisting, nonreactive, to let life flow through one while at the same time remaining aware and intelligent about what is happening: a very different attitude from that of the seeker following the path of orthodoxy, which is the expression of the ordinary, discursive levels of the mind. We hold on to things with clenched fists, or, equally, repudiate them by pushing them aside. The symbolic posture of the hands should be palm upward, the fingers open, both to let go and to receive. Robert Speaight, in one of his novels, speaks tellingly of "the heroism of the relaxed grip." Few people realize that only by such relaxing can the end be achieved. Nor do they appreciate that it needs courage to let go of all one's preconceptions, fixed habits of thought, feeling and the rest. Yet *it is the very act of emptying the mind of what has accumulated in it which is the crucial one,* leading to a major change in oneself, revolutionizing one's attitude to life.

Instead of resisting or trying to change the world, including one's own character, we need a sense that everything, whether its immediate effect is to bring pleasure or pain, even to destroy one's life, is woven into a tapestry with meaningful pattern in every detail. Events take place according to their own laws, and we ourselves are enmeshed in those laws. Nothing is fortuitous, nothing is accidental in the colloquial sense of that word. The fact that we are present when something occurs means that we are part of the over-all event, whether or not we have any active part to play in it. Often, these events are outside our direct control: such things as natural cataclysms, and for most of us, social and political events. Yet if we were not, by the laws of existence, involved, we should be elsewhere, or living in another age.

In other words, every instant of time and every event are our teachers. Our task, if we are trying to reach Essential understanding, is to try to see what this means to us as individuals, what lesson we have to learn from it. We discover that we ourselves have created, projected from ourselves, the pattern which surrounds us. But then comes a further step: it is obvious that if we have already created a situation, we are in a position to go on creating — indeed, we have to do so; and so, if we become sufficiently intelligent about life, we can direct this creation in whatever way we will.

This seems to have a direct relation to a still further stage, one which is exemplified a number of times in quotations given in Huxley's *The Perennial Philosophy*. Here visionaries and saints exclaim to God such things as, "O Thou I," and in other less quaint ways realize that they themselves are the only God there is; but He is *in His completeness,* also to be found in every other "I" and indeed in every particle of matter in the universe. It is not a fragment of Himself but the completeness of Himself which is there, here and now.

It takes a poet to realize this, a poet or any other true artist or seer: but it can also become apparent to the scientist if he can outgrow his science and see what lies beyond it, perhaps in a future science which will be to the present form what an advanced university course is to a kindergarten. The direction of consciousness is, clearly, out of the present level of existence toward something which involves the supreme sacrifice: that of dethroning the discursive, instinct-animated mind which we have developed over millennia, and giving precedence to another aspect of itself which seems utterly contradictory to it. In the process, we have to allow the dissolution of ourselves as egos, the death of individuality which must take place before it can be reborn, transformed and risen from a death which is no less real for being the precursor of the new state of Being.

Chapter XVI

CHRISTIANITY AND THE CHURCHES

The late Professor Paul Tillich, already referred to several times, in the first of a series of lectures given at the University of California, Santa Barbara, set out with great clarity his religious philosophy. Summed up, it was to the effect that religion in the larger sense was "concern for Ultimates," or "Ultimate Concern." But in a lesser sense, *a* religion was a corporate body of men and women united in order to consider Ultimates and seek them out. At least, that is the avowed purpose; but such a body is beset by a universal tendency to fall away from its goal and to acquire characteristics similar to those of every human institution. The kind of mental entropy already mentioned tends to operate in it and results in the development of set creeds, observances, rules, orthodoxy and its complement, heresy; and with this there is a tendency to exalt personalities over principles. Such a thing occurs anywhere, whether in a political party or a tennis club; and a church is no exception. In most cases it is not crucial if this happens, but when it bedevils a body which is supposed to have Ultimate Concern, the result is a process of what Tillich called "demonizing" and growth of idolatry. Idolatry is to give ultimate value to things which are not ultimate, be these rules and rites, customs or certain people. The result is that the Ultimate becomes lost sight of, and what should be the quest for it is reduced to mechanical mental or physical habits. Later, in answer to a student who asked whether one should then leave one's inadequate church, Tillich said "No," adding that he himself remained in his denomination, as a *protestant,* constantly urging the need to look only for Ultimates, and so to destroy idolatry.

It is from this standpoint that we have to consider the problem of organized religion. We can translate Tillich's terminology into that used in this book: "Ultimate Concern" is the search for Being. Idolatry is to lose sight of Being and to return to existence and the conflicting elements which belong to it. Ultimate Concern is to see the Universal, the Eternal, the Noumenal behind the temporal, local and phenomenal. It is Religion as against the supposedly religious.

Wherever we look, moreover, we find a duality between those who remember and seek for the Ultimate, and those who live at the idolatrous level. It is obvious in Hinduism, Buddhism, Islam, Judaism and Christianity in equal measure if in different forms, as well as in societies and groups where membership may cut across named religions in favor of some form of occultism or esotericism. The "idolators" may be entirely sincere, devoted people, let it be said; their lives may often indeed be much the better for having a tangible creed, but nevertheless they lack the sense of the transcendental which ultimately they must find, if they are to move on toward the consciousness of Being. It is often more than superstition which moves the simple peasant to go on a pilgrimage or to put flowers at the foot of a statue of Our Lady, to put a wreath on the neck of Siva's Bull, or light a lamp in a Buddhist shrine. The religious impulse is there but it is inchoate, often undirected toward the genuine Ultimate. This thing in mankind is among its more endearing traits, and often has a deeply touching beauty, however crude its manifestations. That it can and should eventually lead to a more direct and intelligent form of worship is evident, but it is premature to expect it where an individual has not yet awaked to the need to go beyond the forms to which he has become accustomed.

All that has been said applies to every religion, but Christianity has done a peculiar thing. In no other of the major religions is it so generally taught that enlightenment depends on faith in a certain individual, and that only through him can "salvation" be attained. The Buddhists pay great reverence to Gotama, but He is the Enlightener, not Himself the Savior. In Islam, Mohammed is the chief of many prophets including Jesus of Nazareth, but it is not by deifying Mohammed that the Muslim finds his way to paradise.

In Christianity however, there is an extraordinary telescoping of universal and mythological truth with time and history, much to the detriment of the deeper meaning. Every religion has its demonized, idolatrous aspect, but Christianity has excelled itself in pinning down essential and universal verities to supposedly historical and geographical events. No other religion has done this, apart perhaps from some of the primitive remnants of precivilization where the gods (often distinguished from God as a transcendental Absolute) are seen as inhabiting springs, mountains, and caves.

A canon of the Anglican Church once, in the course of discussion, summed up his creed with surprising naiveté: God created the world; something went wrong with it, so he sent his Son to put things right. The fact that there have been other great Teachers such as Krishna, Gotama, Hermes Trismegistus did not seem to him to have any importance. Moreover, what he expected was that in order to be redeemed from original sin, all that the individual need do was to offer his sins to Jesus, and all would be well. No other religion grovels before God or dwells so constantly on sin and sorrow, making of religion a pure misery.

Apart from the crudity of such a notion, one which is the basis of belief in many Christian churches, one cannot but wonder how this whole idea grew up. It is certainly not taught in the Gospels though some of the parables and the admonition to "Follow me" can, by an effort, be reduced to this level by ignoring the deeper implications they so obviously contain. But the excommunication of Gnosticism in the early days of Christianity deprived the Church of its "protestant" schools, which also represented the connection with the thread of esoteric Mystery tradition. The result is, over the centuries, a steadily increasing materialism, a loss of the Noumenal aspects of the Christian formulation of the Perennial and Essential Religion.

Fortunately, today many people are waking up to this and reacting against it. Some frankly disavow the whole Christian dispensation and seek elsewhere. Others ask awkward questions such as whether the appearance of God's supposed only Son on a minor planet extends his redemptive grace to other globes and even stars, where also something like humanity may have "fallen". For, obviously, if the whole universe is God's creation, such an act on his part must perforce be universal and cosmic;

whereas if it applied to the earth alone, it could not be a supreme and absolute Being who performed it, but a local, parochial deity, a god such as one finds in the despised pantheons of paganism. Moreover, it is felt by some that the Dead Sea Scrolls, whose impact is only beginning to be felt, may upset a great deal of supposed history and undermine the foundation of the orthodox Christian church. Further, modern knowledge of comparative religion and anthropology shows us how much paganism has been absorbed into the worship and hagiology of the churches.

Then another and still more basic question may be raised. We are constantly told that the Bible is the Word of God: that in it we have a direct revelation of what he intends for mankind. But on what authority other than habit and tradition does this assertion rest? Why should the Bible be taken more — or less — seriously than, say, the *Vedas,* the *Bhagavad-Gita,* the *Tao Teh King* and other ancient scriptures? And if Jesus were to return to the world, as is expected, but otherwise than with the trappings of the legend of the Last Judgment, is it not likely that he himself would be so different from the idea built up in the minds of most Christians that the popes and bishops and theologians would, as the Jews did earlier, not only fail to see what he was, but brand him as a heretic and his own Antichrist? In other words, the church image of the Christ today is a "demonized" and idolatrous one, far removed from the Essential reality of what he is.

There is, however, a growing movement away from this. It began long before the Qumran manuscripts and others of similar origin were found. Albert Schweitzer wrote a scholarly book analyzing the Gospels and what historical evidence there is about the time when Jesus is supposed to have lived. His conclusion is that, though there was almost surely a Teacher sometime about the supposed beginning of our era, we know nothing about his physical life. The Gospels are not history but myth, and what we are apt to treat as telling of events in time, is in fact the timeless story of man's perfectibility, everywhere, and at every period in history. In other words, we can agree with Schweitzer that if we remove the Jesus of the Gospels from any events on the material level and see him as the hero of the myth of the spiritual development of awakened man. no denial of history touches Christianity or invalidates its true meaning.

Otherwise put, we can only benefit by abandoning the attempt to fit the Gospels into a material framework, and by linking them up with other forms of the same myth such as exist in Freemasonry, Rosicrucianism, alchemy, as well as in pre-Christian paganism and in non-Christian religions. It only strengthens Christianity to see it as part of a universal and perennial tradition which cannot be upset. If the Teacher of Righteousness of the Dead Sea Scrolls should turn out to have been the historical Jesus, and even if a historical Passion is found never to have taken place, Christianity goes on, probably all the better for having lost its materialism.

It becomes possible, using modern knowledge, to restore and resurrect the profound and beautiful truths of Christianity, so that it can become a living faith for scientists and intellectuals as much as for simple people. To do so means taking a new look at the myth which has gathered round whatever actual teacher there was, somewhere about two thousand years ago in Palestine. Gotama, the Buddha, lived in India some centuries earlier and taught the Way in a manner suitable to the time and place. Jesus, called the Christ, taught the same Way in a Judaeo-Greco-Roman form also suited to the times and the cultural background. And for us, living in our Judaeo-Christian world, it should have a special appeal; but we need to see its Essential quality clearly, to rid ourselves of most of the existentially derived theology and its materialistic setting.

We may take the one called Jesus as Everyman, or Bunyan's Pilgrim: our own selves, seeking to reach the level of Being and to know God directly. We can follow the story as a simple thread running through the Gospels, with excursions into parable and sermon, as it were on the side. The latter contain teachings comparable with those of other spiritual Teachers. But, as Jesus constantly reminds us, they need to be understood properly and not merely literally.

The theme of the Gospels begins at that point where a man — any man — feels the first touch of Being, has the first "peak experience." Jesus has this first impulse at his mythological

110

birth in the humility of the stable, the "cave of the heart." Without going into detail, we then see the Pilgrim go through various stages, each standing for an expansion of consciousness, a widening of the door into Being, an initiation: the Baptism, the Transfiguration, the Passion, the Resurrection and the Ascension, then as an aftermath, the special outpouring typified by Whitsun, the final consummation of his role as at once true God and true man, becoming the anointed Christos.

Of all these, the Passion is perhaps the most poignant and the most telling for modern man. We have first the entry into Jerusalem, in as much pomp as Jesus ever experienced. Could it be that the popular acclaim of Palm Sunday stirred up in him the last vestiges of pride and personal egoism? If so, he was soon to be purged of them. For in Gethsemane, not only was he deserted by his closest friends and followers, he underwent the humiliation of failing himself. He said in effect "I can't take any more, I cannot do what is expected of me." He goes through the subsequent events a self-defeated man with no personal pride left, sustained only by his sense that "It is written, it is part of the pattern." There is, indeed can be, no trace of resentment now even against those who treated him worst. The death on the symbolic Cross closes that chapter of an ordeal which is inevitable on the path of holiness and self-fulfillment, and which is the ineluctable precursor to rebirth and the new state of Being, the goal of human endeavor, the self-destruction of Nietzsche — Nirvana. This consummation can only be reached by the man who has experienced and accepted existence fully. He has not tried to escape from its conflicts and suffering; but by saying, in a sense, "So be it," he finds himself on the threshold of what he seeks. Finally, on the cross, he finds God has deserted him: but he himself goes on, becomes his own God.

Seen in this way, without emotionalism and sentimentality, we have in the Gospels something which applies to each one who sets out to find out what life means. It is the same with Arjuna in the *Bhagavad-Gita,* though quite differently expressed. True meaning is not to be found in the material world, that of existence, of *yin-yang* arrayed in battle in opposition to one another. But every time a man accepts the pain which arises from conflict, lifts himself into a real and positive acceptance of

111

it, he has, in a small way, undergone the ordeal of the Passion and been reborn, in however small a degree. Man undergoes endless minor crucifixions in his career through life. Maybe, indeed if we are to believe the Seers, these lesser passions lead up to a final and major one, after which the individual is himself a Christos, a charismatic person in the fullest sense. That is, he becomes a link between the divine, Noumenal levels of Being and the people who are still enmeshed in the phenomena of existence, an incarnation or *avatar* of the basic Archetype, God. Long before this, however, an individual can, through the Christian *mythos,* and through the other main channels of the religions, or even without adopting and adapting to himself any of these, be gradually "reborn" and change his ways and attitudes to life as he goes on. In some measure we see this happening in many people today as they look for the new conscious level they feel they must reach in order to live as they should.

Some may become more quietistic, more Quaker-like. They may feel they cannot honestly go to churches where hate, vengeance and misery rather than love and joy are preached; and even when they find themselves expected to say that "there is no health in me," the sense of inner dignity and of the divine in them may make them rebel, because it is not true. Indeed, as one person put it, he was so profoundly Christian that he could not take part in most services, and so kept away.

This justifiable attitude, however, had the disadvantage of depriving him of what is to be found in congregational worship. This, unless it should really be an obstacle to an individual at a stage where he should be more concerned with inward contemplation, can help in two ways. First, to join a group in a common act and a common purpose, invokes the dynamics of coalescence of individual minds around the same ideal. The strength of that mind is greater than the sum of its parts and helps the individual in his aspirations. Second, as we have said, valid ritual is the dramatic playing-out of myth, with the chief officiants clad in traditional regalia intended to mask the individual personality behind the archetypal role. The role itself, if the ceremony is performed with proper intent and understanding, brings its own charismatic quality into the whole. The drama itself, moreover, is usually linked with ancient tradition in which there is an unbroken line whereby this archetypal role is handed on from generation to generation, as in the Apostolic Succession of the Catholic and Orthodox Churches. Moreover, the Christian tradition embodies throughout the year a series of progressive variations on the main theme, which links it with the seasons and with what are clearly, extensions of rites practised long before the Christian era.

Such ceremonies — and they need not be Christian; Freemasonry, under its eighteenth century pomposity, is mythologically valid, as are some other rites — play the same role in external life as does the study of mythological dreams in the inner. They may, even if the outer form is imperfect and in some measure corrupt, evoke even today a living experience of Being in the one who takes part in them intelligently or with true devotion. The Mass and Communion are often the channel of profound numinous experience.

It is however for the individual to find out for himself how best to pursue his own search. Moreover, he should not hesitate to do things differently at different periods. The fact that certain things have been done in a certain way for generations does not of necessity mean that it is good to continue them today; nor does antiquity, however, mean that change is imperative. What matters is that life and consciousness of Being should flow into a person. What Christians call Grace needs to come out of Being and to be received by the existential mind as it aspires toward the Real, in whatever form and through whatever channel it comes. We have in this chapter emphasized the Judaeo-Christian side because it is the background of the west, or has been until now, when east and west tend to mingle, to the benefit of both. There is great need, especially in Christianity, to try to separate the material and historical from the eternal and universal, and to emphasize the much greater importance of the latter even if the supposed history should be factually correct; and equally to show how the truth of Christianity remains unshaken if it is not. Truth can be found even if one begins at a narrow, sectarian level. For if an individual is really seeking it, the search itself will lead to a widening of understanding in which consciousness will spill out beyond the narrow channel of dogmas and creeds. A "church Christian" may thus make a start in his sect and, as he grows, discover the glories of pure Christian, or Buddhist, or other teachings.

We thus have two main ways for a Christian to seek God and the state of Being which follows when God is found. In one, he acts out myth in ritual and observance, in the other the same mythical drama unfolds subjectively, inside the psyche. In one, Jacob's ladder is seen as outside onself, in the other it is inside. The same archetypal angelic forms move up and down. Eventually, both converge at the same point — in Being. There such terms as *yin* and *yang,* subjective and objective, cease to have separate meaning, resolved in the numinous quality of God or Tao, the Universal and Absolute Reality.

As an epilogue to this section, here is a brief note on prayer, since this is one of the cardinal practices advocated in the churches. A great deal that is excellent has been written about this, while there is also much which amounts to begging, or telling God how to run His universe. One has even heard of someone who prayed that her bridge-playing might be improved by divine intervention. In other cases the petition is for forgiveness, with a promise to make a sacrifice. Both petitionary and placatory prayer clearly belong to the existential level of the mind, and are addressed to the god who is opposed to, and by, a shadow figure, the devil.

The Essential prayer is communion with the true God. It is not of necessity verbal, but expresses itself in awe, wonder, love, and joy. To contemplate and experience in a certain way is the prayer of one who has a sense of the Numinous. He does not ask for anything. This was formulated by one who said, in effect, "God, I pray that when I meet Thee face to face, I shall have the courage to ask nothing of Thee." And a Muslim saint in North Africa, speaking to an agnostic French doctor, summed the matter up to the effect that if you do not *know* and *feel* your unity with God, you should pray. If you know your own divinity, you no longer have that need.

One who has once established in himself the sense of the Numinous, who is sufficiently self-aware and awake, can be said to be at prayer all through the day — and probably the night too. His mind will be turned in a certain direction and, even if it deviates and sometimes forgets, it will tend to return to its proper orientation as soon as it removes its attention from the situation in which his little ego has become involved. Such a state renders any other need obsolete. Moreover, the constant return, if not to the actual Source of Being, at least to the intuition of it, brings one closer to that Source without a word spoken. This gradually changes the discursive, personal mind by illuminating it from within: and that is the purpose of all Religion.

Chapter XVII

PHYSICAL LIFE AND DEATH

One of the few things about which we can be quite certain is that, sooner or later, our bodies will die. What, if anything, happens after death is a subject which can be debated *ad infinitum.* Some claim to know the details of an after-life; some categorically deny it; all are equally ignorant. Others couple the idea of cycles, their sense of the invisible world of mind and the still less time-embroiled one of Essence, and accept, if only in general terms, the idea of some kind of repeated incarnations. But this opens up the question as to whether the reincarnating entity bears any recognizable features of one who has died, whether similar personality traits persist, or whether what is reborn is only the Essential, timeless Self of a person. They may even go further and think that while the personal mind may *survive* physical death for a time, it is not *immortal.* What is immortal is the super-personal Being of an individual. In Buddhism unadulterated by less pure doctrines, this view is taken, coupled with the principle that such a Being is in effect brought back to birth willy-nilly by unresolved *skandhas,* or "bundles" of material. Admitting that the western view is an over-simplification of the eastern, these *skandhas* can legitimately be associated with complexes as known to psychologists, remaining unresolved at the time of death and hence still active in the psyche. Whatever a *skandha* may be, this is how it seems to act. It, so to speak, clings to the Essence and is the cause of the individual's being tied to the wheel of time and rebirth. It is only in so far as the personal mind is already pervaded by the Numinous that there is possibly a direct and recognizable connection between the personality at point A on the time-track, the rim of the wheel, and that at a later point, B, also on that rim. Otherwise, the average person, unawakened and without "intimations of immortality" may be said to be immortal only as Essential Being.

Such speculations can be endless without being fruitless because they must affect our attitude toward physical death. The present feeling of most people still is that death is something to be avoided at all cost except perhaps when one sacrifices one's life for others. To them death is tragedy, the end of a book rather than of a chapter. Hence life on earth should be preserved for as long as possible, after which "poor Jones" becomes an object of pity, and his death, one of regret. It matters where his body lies; people refer to him as being in a grave, which can be almost a temple of worship. Doctors are said to be bound by an oath which can be interpreted as an undertaking to consider survival of the body before all else, even the wishes or comfort of the patient. In short, primitive survival instinct is prevalent even among sophisticated people today, and prompts them to practices which, especially in America, are sometimes frankly horrible, and a denial of any sense of true religion or love for the departed.

Cynics may, moreover, point out that it is often not the agnostic and materialist who takes physical death seriously and tragically. It is the pious member of religious sects which teach of an after-life which, except for the unrepentant sinner, becomes at once entirely blissful and glorious.

Attitudes, however, are changing as the germs of the new mind emerge. Already there is a feeling that to battle for life when one is old and perhaps crippled is not after all so heroic and praiseworthy. The action of the doctor who was also a churchwarden, yet fought to save his idiot son so that he survived and occupied the complete time of two attendants, is today apt to be viewed with some doubt, both from the viewpoint of society and of his own attitude toward the value of physical life, especially in such a case. Even judges tend to show some sympathy for the "mercy killer" who helps to end the sufferings of his kinsman. Some of the more intelligent doctors, too, say frankly that in some cases, it is more important to see to the patients' comfort than it is to try to extend physical life for a few days or hours. They are still too few, but it is probable that this attitude is growing even if not openly avowed.

It seems as if, as the sense of the Numinous increases in individuals, their attitude toward death must alter. Temporal existence runs from birth to death, in the physical world at least. From the essential angle, these are clearly as much complementary poles as are night and day. Moreover, they are seen to coexist all through: the body begins to die almost as soon as it is conceived, while the growth-process, which is the extension of the critical event of conception or birth, continues so long as the body lives. At first the growth forces predominate; later those of involution, disintegration leading to death, overtake the former as those forces weaken. Growth and dying are inseparable companions. If one wishes, one may put it that growth is *yang* to deterioration which is *yin* in early life. These poles become reversed as time goes on. In any case, both are equally "good" from the evolutionary and Taoistic viewpoint. When the body dies it simply means that the individual has come to the end of a certain chapter in the total cycle of his evolutionary existence.

Out of this comes the view that physical death is no evil or tragic thing. It is entirely natural and, like other natural processes, is not to be feared. Indeed, it is repeatedly found that even when a person has been afraid of dying, toward the end of his days he opens up inwardly, so that, as his end approaches, he is strangely serene. It is only the onlookers who feel grief and distress, not the dying person himself. Fear or grief over dying arises from identification of the ego with the body. Even people of intelligence often say, "When I die" (if they do not evade the direct phrase, as many do) when what they really mean is, "When my body dies." This shows the tendency of primitive instinct to persist, even if the individual concerned has the belief that he himself will, in some form, not die so much as be released from his physical appendage.

At the same time, such a belief is not necessary either logically or emotionally. Death can be approached calmly without it. One professed agnostic said to a friend, as he lay at death's door, "You believe in an after-life. I don't. If you are right I may be able to come and tell you so. If I am, I obviously shall not." And he went on to point out that if he were, as he thought, going to vanish altogether, it would be illogical to be afraid. On the contrary, wracked with pain, it would be nice to be free; and if he did not survive in any form, there would be no possibility of the suffering going on.

Others, too, have the feeling that when they see the body of some loved person, what is left really has nothing more to do with the individual: it is an empty shell, a discarded suit of clothes, and quite irrelevant to the state of the one who has worn it. As one person put it, after seeing her dead father, "What is lying on the bed is certainly not Father. I don't know where he is, but I am sure he is not in that room." And another, speaking of himself, said to his relatives, "Get rid of my body as quickly as you like, and with a minimum of fuss. I don't care what you do: one thing is sure, that I won't be interested any more, and I won't come to my funeral unless I have to. In any case, and whether or not anything recognizable as me goes on, the sure thing is that a dead body cannot feel or see or in any other way respond to what is done to it. If it could, it would not be dead."

It seems from such remarks as if the growing sense of the invisible world, without in any way of necessity involving any doctrine of survival or extinction, rests on a new sense of the value of physical life. It would be difficult to say just how this may develop as time goes on. But one thing seems certain, that death will become a thing to be taken in stride. We are a long way yet from the place where humanity could be entrusted with the authority to use euthanasia, whether with or without a patient's consent. But our attitude toward living in constant pain or crippled by injuries as against dying seems likely to become more rational as we realize at once the naturalness of death and the fact that it comes at what is for the individual the right Present. There seems to be much in the idea that what Jung calls synchronicity, and the Chinese call Tao, and modern psychologists by some such term as "peak experience" are all connected with the climax of death, and probably also, with conception and birth. The sense of "Now and Here" cannot fail to bring with it freedom from many of our old habits and attitudes of thought and feeling. Notably must this be the case where the temporal phenomena, of which birth and death are climactic moments, are concerned.

119

Chapter XVIII

DISEASE AND MEDICINE

Consideration of the problem of death naturally leads to that of disease. A vast amount of time and energy are spent in trying to prevent and cure illness both of mind and body. This is as it should be; but the matter needs to be considered philosophically if it is to be successful in more than a superficial way. Our usual attitude is that illness is an unmitigated evil and should be eliminated as quickly as may be. But such a wholesale condemnation is a product of the existential mind, and a polar opposite to another extreme view, that God deliberately sends us suffering in order to test our characters and to chasten us for our sins. The new mind will probably evolve an attitude which will integrate both these views against a wider background.

To the Essential mind, disease is nothing fortuitous. It has its place and purpose in our lives and is a sign of unbalance somewhere in our total life pattern. It therefore has something to teach us. In this way the "evil" of it can be transmuted by an act of mind into a "good." It gives an individual an indication that he is out of tune with his teleology and here is a chance to put things right, as well as to grow in awareness.

Georg Groddeck in the twenties provocatively stated that our colloquial way of speaking tells us what happens. We do not say, "X has had his leg broken," but "X has broken his leg," or "caught the measles," implying that he has done these things to himself. Groddeck points out that there are a number of more or less unconscious reasons why we get ill. It may be to avoid an unpleasant situation, possibly ordinary life as a whole. Many a chronic invalid has run away from facing this, the mental retreat coming before any physical deterioration sets in. A sick person often becomes a center of attention: he has power in the household in a way he would not otherwise have. Elizabeth Barrett's health improved when she married Robert Browning and escaped from the dictatorship of her father. We can think of many examples of this kind among our friends, and perhaps even as regards ourselves. We may get ill in order to punish ourselves because we feel guilty. We may have done something we genuinely repent, or the guilt may be of the false variety caused by the Freudian super-ego; but the result is the same. Groddeck has perhaps over-simplified things. Chronic disease especially may serve as a permanent refuge for somebody who feels that she has been cornered by life. Granted that she may have created her own trap, she makes no further effort until she has realized what she is doing, or until something happens (such as the death of a bullying husband) to change the circumstances. Beyond this, too, there is the purpose served by sickness in enforcing idleness and giving rest. In this it can be of use in much the same way as the Catholic's retreat, not a defeat, but a period given over to contemplation, meditation and prayer, with a view to coming closer to one's spiritual roots. Illness can then be a time of rebirth and regeneration.

Jung carries the matter still further when he argues that all dis-ease (the word is hyphenated so that it includes all kinds of discomfort, including social maladjustment, lack of education or opportunity, and the rest) is a sign that one is somewhere astray from one's spiritual path, the *dharma* of Hinduism and Buddhism. The symptom is a warning signal on the road, and should be heeded. Hence, the responsibility for one's troubles, despite whatever help one may receive from others, lies within oneself; and, as a rider to this, so does the healing which brings about readjustment to life. There is much in the Christian Scientists' idea that if one is ill one is "in error," though the corollary, that illness should be ignored as non-existent, is false: it does exist and, consequently, should be frankly faced and the root cause sought. If one does not seek it, though one set of symptoms may vanish, another is likely to replace it.

Seen in this way, disease may be tackled intelligently and positively. Evil from one angle, it is good from another. It becomes good when it brings the individual into line, not with the social morality of the super-ego, but with his own true inner sense of what is right for himself, as an individual among other individuals. In this way, *disease is a healing process* in the wider perspective of total life. It brings one nearer to the "wholeness," holiness or integration which is the teleological aim of every individual, however much his existential personality may rebel.

From what we have said, it might seem that when a person is ill no attempt should be made to help him, that for doctor or nurse to do anything would be an intrusion into the privacy of his individual life. But if there is any truth in the principle that one's environment is a reflection of his inner state, it is clear that the fact that a healer finds himself in that environment, or is called into it, makes him a part of it. Equally, the situation becomes a reflected aspect of oneself, so that the two existential personalities, sick man and doctor, are linked and interacting. Each one has something to do for the other, and the measures taken by the doctor play into whatever can be evoked from the patient. The whole process is a two-way catalysis. This is particularly the case when the principal therapy is at the mental level. Jung points out that to do good work in psychotherapy, the therapist has to commit himself to the dialogue with the patient as fully as the patient himself. Each influences and can enrich and teach the other, though the therapist should have some start on the patient, and be further on the road to integration if he is to be effective. If he is not, the whole process is inclined to run into a vicious circle; while, equally, if the therapist's ego feels itself to be superior to his patient's, no real contact will be established. There can then be little else than the tendency to a morbid "transference" whereby the patient bcomes emotionally dependent on the very one to whom he has come in search of psychic freedom.

Things can only be seen in this light by doctor or nurse when they have, albeit inarticulately, some sense of the deeper aspects of life beyond the existential. If a therapist has this sense, he will be more effective than a more intellectually brilliant individual who does not have it. This is why the district nurse or the old-fashioned country doctor is, as we have said earlier, often a better healer than the highly qualified specialist. He will be in the true sense a spiritual healer, be he doctor, nurse, dentist, masseur or vet. He does not need to lay on hands, though he may do so. Needless to say he should never feel personal pride in his work, or look upon himself as a superior and specially endowed individual. If he does, his personal ego must inevitably stand in the way, and the spiritual charisma fails. Perhaps the best summary of the position is that of Canon Harold Anson. His book on spiritual healing, published about 1920, says in effect that spiritual healing can come only through a spiritual person. But it will do so then, whatever his calling, and whether this is in the direct therapeutic field or not.

The actual work of the surgeon, the physician, the manipulator, is clearly at the "lower" or existential level, while the essential, spiritual factor comes in from another dimension. It does so *when it is allowed to,* just as water or air will flow through any channel open to it. In this sense, healing is permissive rather than active. This applies to the patient as much as to the doctor. Basically, healing is the setting free of what has been called *vis medicatrix naturae,* the healing force of nature. The spiritual healer is one who succeeds in evoking from the patient such a reaction as will allow nature to do her work. All healing is "natural." True, an unwise physician may slow the process by the use of too many, or the wrong, medicines; but the wise one, with a good clinical sense (an intuitive, not an intellectual faculty) will use his pharmacy to ease the patient and so to give him the best chance of finding his own health. Several decades ago Dr. Maxwell Telling, professor of pharmacology in Leeds University, used to say that healing consisted in rest and nursing, a suitable diet, and the use of drugs, (his own special field of work) in that order. In this way, he said, he could do possibly no better than a "nature cure" practitioner but he could do it much quicker, with more certainty, and less risk. This it may be added, was long before the discovery of antibiotics, which have introduced a new element into therapy one one which, in its novelty, is being much misused. Yet there are already signs that a more balanced approach is returning, and that many old-fashioned remedies are coming back into vogue. This, and the emphasis on teaching students to think of "the whole patient" and the insistence that no amount of chemical and other tests can replace "clinical sense" are entirely on the right lines for the future. This clinical sense must of course involve the Cinderella of medicine, only too slowly coming into the curriculum and into the minds of doctors, which is to realize the power of the mind even in physical disease. And, of course, few have any clear idea of the deepest aspect of man, the Essential.

All this suggests a clue as to the attitude of the doctor or other therapist to his work. He cannot be at once both egotistical and spiritual. On the contrary, the best people in the field are essentially humble, unassuming. Even the sense that so many healers have, that they are chosen by God, or that God wants them to take up the work, is a stumbling block. The true therapist needs to be very impersonal, detached from his patients — but not isolated in the way we have spoken of earlier — deeply loving yet completely undemanding of anything in return. These seemingly contradictory matters are not so in reality when seen from the super-personal or Essential level. They represent what is meant by *empathy* as distinct from *sympathy*. Sympathy, desirable as it is, may be defined as being an external link between two personalities, a harmonious relationship. But empathy stands for a deeper quality and, as the word indicates, it is *sympathy from within*. It derives from the sense of Essential unity with another. While sympathy belongs to the personal realm, empathy is beyond or above this level; hence it is non-reactive to what the other person is or does. It is a complete acceptance of him without, however, any sentimental pandering to him. This seems to be the basic quality of the true healer, if he is sufficiently enlightened to be able to achieve it.

This essay cannot ignore the very rare recorded cases where it seems that a miracle has occurred and a sick person has been healed where, in a sense, no healing could take place. We have not only tradition, including the Gospel stories, but even today there are some instances which are attested to in a manner which

124

satisfies modern critical standards. Lourdes affords a few. Among the millions who have visited the shrine, a few score have found relief from real organic disease. It is worth noting that clinical notes show that both Dorothy Kerin* and Carrel's girl at Lourdes had similar diseases, were ardent Christians, and that both afterwards turned to healing work. The important factor here seems to be this capacity for dedication to the service of others. It seems to indicate that at the time of the cures the patients were in some way inwardly attuned, so that more than usual power seemed to be released in them. Whether or not the supposed agent of the cure was a person called Jesus or Our Lady, is secondary: it might have been what the patients believed or it might equally be a dramatized archetypal image fitting in with the personal myth. The crucial matter is that it happened, and that the evidence is beyond reasonable doubt.

This prompts the question as to why it is only in rare cases that such strange happenings occur. The majority of pilgrims to Lourdes carry their diseases home with them; but out of the crowd a fair number go away with a new attitude to life, to themselves, and to their illness. This more willing acceptance of things-as-they-are rather than resentment or self-pity that things are not as they would like them to be, is itself a half-miracle. Something has happened which had not happened before, and it seems to have been unchained by the *mana* or charisma of the place or person visited. It may be added that there are probably many more miraculous cures than one ever hears about. The "healer" in such cases remains obscure and does not seek publicity for something with which he may feel in a sense unconcerned, a very different attitude from that of the self-advertising figures whose results it is difficult ever to confirm.

Why then are not miracles much more frequent? The answer can only be that the inner attitude of the patient is at fault: demanding rather than accepting, closed and fixed, not open, however pious and devoted he may seem from the outside.

We have today a *corpus* of medicine which is very valuable and which contains much that is good. The average practitioner constantly helps to bring about cures: nobody pays any attention

*See *The Living Touch* by Dorothy Kerin and others, and *Journey to Lourdes* by Alexis Carrel.

to them. But if he makes a mistake the press is only too anxious to report the matter. in contrast to this — and it speaks for itself — a failure by a "fringe" practitioner gets little publicity, but a success may well do so.

This body of medical knowledge, however imperfect, is the product of man's mind up to the present. It is therefore suited to the contemporary scene, and for better or worse has to be accepted as such. On the other hand, since everything must progress and cannot stand still, not only must this *corpus* itself change — as it is changing — from within, it needs also to allow contemporary trends to become incorporated in it. In particular, this can be brought about not only through research at the existential level, but also by taking into account the view of man as a spiritual being.

A vital part of the change, too, is to be looked for in this deeper view of the human being. Science today is playing with ideas which might lead to results in every way as devastating as any bomb. There is talk of changing humanity by controlling heredity, sex and the like, bringing about desirable mutations. This is based on a misconception, in which man is identified with his body. Bodily changes, however, have no direct effect on the Essential man, nor, except indirectly, on man as a personality centered in the mind. Cripple his body, and his mind is what it was, even if it can no longer express itself through that body. At most, he suffers mentally by being starved of the interchange between himself and his environment; and, while such restriction is, if the principles of this book are right, a part of his immediate pattern in life, self-produced, self-projected, the Essential man remains and can profit by the painful lot of his outer life.

From the Essential angle, therefore, to try to upset the balance of nature where man is concerned is likely to produce physical results which are inconceivably monstrous and distorted. It is at the mental level of the mental animal, man, (where evolution seems to be focused today) that valid results can be obtained. To be in the greater sense good and progressive, therapy as well as illness should, both directly and indirectly, lead to increased awareness and toward permanent experience of the Essential.

On the plane of actual practice, we may well see in the future a revival of the old, charismatic role of the doctor who is also a priest. His priesthood will not depend on belonging to a specific body of men and women, such as obtained of old, but on his own inner consciousness and the charismatic qualities which this gives him. The doctor today is still inclined to behave as if he were a high priest; but his god tends to be more himself and his profession, than the spiritual quality which is in his patient as much as in himself. The result is that his personal ego stands in the way of the deeper healing. Moreover, he resents anything which challenges the edifice of orthodox medicine. We may hope to see develop a different attitude, where superstition and pseudo-science will be sifted for any truth in them before being discarded, even if it means that the frontiers of science have to be shifted to include them.

Such priest-doctors may work then in the kind of "polyclinic" which existed at Epidauros and in the other temples of Asklepios, brought up to date by modern science, but without rejecting the invisible and the Numinous. Indeed, this latter will be the focus of the work, all personal needs being referred to it. There are already signs that, here and there, both in the Christian and the non-Christian communities a beginning is being made, but not publicized or advertised.

In conclusion, while it is premature to foreshadow the course of medicine in the future, present indications point in the direction of a deeper and more intelligent, as well as more scientific view of illness. Man is seen in a context; his mind is being accepted as real, not a phantasm with no existence of its own. The "art" is slowly returning to its proper place beside the "science" of medicine, and gradually the field is widening so as to take in whatever is valid in what is now called "fringe medicine" — many of the methods nowadays largely exploited by honest cranks and perhaps less honest charlatans.

Chapter XIX

LIMITATIONS

The world of existence is finite. In every direction except that of imagination — which, when properly used and not debased into fantasy, links up with that of Being — one sooner or later comes to a point beyond which he cannot go. In the physical world, as this point is approached, the difficulties of further progress mount, not in arithmetical but in geometrical proportion. We find, for example, in the science of cryogenics, or frost-production, that every fraction of a degree nearer to the theoretically calculated Absolute Zero, (—273° Centigrade, nearly but never actually reached) demands an effort perhaps a million times greater than is needed to raise or lower temperature between that of boiling water and ice. Examples of the same kind can be found everywhere.

This means that, from the viewpoint of man on this earth, there seems to be a range of norms, and the further we move from these norms the more difficult and the rarer things become. Research and achievement are always uphill work; but while the gradient may be slight to begin with, the further one goes, the steeper it becomes, until gravity and the forces which try to overcome it balance. Here, an end is reached, and further movement along the same line ceases.

In saying this in any specific instance, however, it is wise to be cautious. Our ancestors said that many things, such as flight, wireless communications and endless other things commonplace today, were impossible, or else "had no future" in their application to ordinary life. Moreover, there is often a "breakthrough" where, by using some new principle, work can continue through what seemed impenetrable obstacles: radar is rapidly conquering fog in sea and air navigation; X-rays have long since shown us things otherwise invisible; electronics have extended the range of microscopy, as they have also outclassed optical telescopes. Yet invariably there is the point where the very nature of the physical world says "Stop." Until we near that barrier, however, human progress in the conquest of the external world proceeds apace, and there are many lines on which no end is in sight.

In other research fields, however, it is already quite clear that there is a limit to man's activity. If we consider the human frame, it is surprising how much it can endure in the way of heat, cold, starvation and the like, but when it comes to gravitational stresses and weightlessness, only a minority can stand up to forces which would seriously damage the average man or woman. By using the external environment, as man has done since the beginning of time, he can add to his activities by using clothing and artificial conditions like heating, cooling, pressurizing, air conditioning, to keep the external world at bay. But it is obvious how cumbersome life then becomes, and also how restricted man's liberty of action.

More speculative yet no less interesting is another level which science has not yet considered. Fear and loneliness are obvious enough stresses on the minds of astronauts. But, as we reach farther out into space, apart from radiation or collision hazards, it seems possible that man may find himself overwhelmed by non-physical yet external conditions which might disrupt his mind as well as affect the subtler vital integrity of his body.

There is another possible aspect of things even on the surface of the earth. It is known that certain people are affected by electromagnetic changes around rapidly moving objects such as meteorites or the ultrasonic V2 rockets of the last war (see chapter XII). No ill effects have so far been noted as having been produced by these despite the nervous and sensory response. But the fact that the organism reacts at all to them opens up the possibility that some people might be unable to travel in supersonic aircraft where they would, even in an enclosed capsule, be under the influence of electro-magnetic effects for several hours on end.

These are not attempts to prophesy, nor is there any *scientific* reason for expecting these effects. But the student of depth psychology, and particularly of parapsychology, has already enough fragmentary material for speculation on these lines to be within reason.

So far we have emphasized only external factors which are likely to limit our researches. They are inescapable. But there are others which are less definite because they depend on the inner workings of the mind. They are of greater concern to this book, and they may put a stop to certain forms of work long before the external obstacles make themselves felt. Given a certain outlook, they may impose a negative which is far more categorical and imperative than any outer consideration. They arise, not from factual, scientific and intellectual reactions. They are more in the nature of feeling than of logic, and rather than anything else represent a sense of values.

Feeling, as we have suggested, operates in two main fields. In that of existence it is emotion, but in that of Being its quality is stillness; and, moreover, it is allied to the extension of ordinary thinking into its new, Essential form rather than, as in the case of emotion, often in opposition to rationality. It is perhaps unfortunate that so far, many impulses which are in line with what we believe to be Essential principles are so much infused with emotion that they frustrate themselves, and even arouse the obstinacy of the scientist in persisting in certain directions. This persistence — also emotional — rests on the assumption that extended knowledge is always good, and justifies the means of obtaining it, as also that what seems to be for the benefit of human beings is more important than damage to any other creature. In both directions, true and balanced sensitivity is blunted and essential Rightness is difficult to discern.

We see this today particularly in relation to animals, which are exploited as if they had neither rights nor the capacity to suffer; though such suffering may be and often is much exaggerated by the more sentimental, who forget the benefits which accrue when animals are domesticated and fed and cared for by man. It is difficult today to determine how much is ethically permissible and where experiment and exploitation should cease. Yet cease it must at a certain point.

Where the human being is concerned, it may well be that the present difficulties in the way of major transplantation of organs will be at least largely overcome. So far the failures outnumber the successes, but this may not always be so. Yet while one must admire the technical skill shown in such operations, from a deeper level than that of mechanics one has to share the unease which shows in the minds of some physicians and intelligent laymen especially when they discuss (in 1969) such things as transplants of hearts, or the tampering with genetic material. The latter especially opens up the possibility that the Frankenstein story might become a monstrous reality. Is it permissible to treat a living body like a machine, replacing worn out organs by better ones in order to prolong life? The organs, in any case, cannot be turned on a lathe or grown in a jar: they have to be taken from what is left of another entity who may sometimes willingly offer such an organ as a kidney, but cannot voice his objections to losing his heart because he is dead or, as some wonder, *may* be dead yet possibly is not. (Such a process is known in engineering as "cannibalizing" and the term seems apt, the purpose being the same where a body is concerned whether that body be eaten or incorporated uneaten into another.)

Then the question arises as to how much of a person's body could be replaced by pieces of another's before he ceases to be the individual one knows, losing his identity in a conglomerate of elements belonging to another. This point is debatable both from the angle of materialism and of the Essential mind. For to the materialist the body is the man — yet he proposes to confuse one man's body with that of others; whereas to the Essential mind the body is not the man but his vehicle, so could be held to be unimportant until we go still further, and see the physical body as in every way as important as the subtler aspects of the individual — a point we shall discuss in the next chapter.

The one who tries to see matters from the angle of Being will perhaps wonder whether to prolong a life by heroic methods is not unwarranted interference with the rhythms of a person's wider life. The latter includes also his death at a time which is, from this viewpoint, right for him.* The problem is, again, one of balance. Nobody would question the duty of giving artificial respiration to a

---

*The famous British physician, Lord Horder, commenting on the supposed Hippocratic Oath said that he accepted the fact that the physician's duty was to preserve life; but that it was not his duty to prolong the agony of dying. This seems a sensible and truly ethical attitude illustrating the practice of many a good doctor. The only matter left open to his judgment is that of when death or the act of dying begins, as begin it must at some time.

drowned person if one happens to be able to do so. But where should one stop resuscitational methods? Murder is unethical, but may not matters eventually go so far as to create a new crime, "anti-murder," equally to be deprecated?

It is a welcome sign to find people today already questioning the old shibboleths that it is always the doctors' duty to preserve life at any cost, even in a mutilated or mindless body; and also that we should pursue knowledge at the possible expense of wisdom, which may be crowded out by accumulation of too many facts.

It is, clearly, very difficult to lay down rules as if they were based on the deeper vision of a higher mentality. Such a mind is embryonic still, even in the most thoughtful, and can only suggest that every case presents its own problems and has to be taken separately. Preceding experience is then used only to foresee the likely outcome.

In general, too, the new mind seems likely to bring about a return to a simpler and less frenzied form of daily living. At present we find money, luxury, "fun," exhibitionism — the cult of the beauty queen, of "glamor" (a word that means a form of deception) — prestige, "face," all being given more importance, at times, than the things which really matter to the human kind. If these fall back into their proper place and people ask only for reasonable amenity, and the leisure which can be used creatively — which does not mean of necessity *doing* so much as *being* — the whole pattern of life must change. Not least of the major items in this, too, must be the economic system. This is based on the success of the parrot cry "Produce more, sell more, demand more!" There might then not be the demand for so many goods; and profit and industry would become the servant, not the master of the State. And the State itself might react from competitive nationalism and rivalry toward a more united sense of world citizenship and to a lowering of the barriers which nowadays split us up and enclose us in our various concentration camps.

There is much we cannot foresee, but it is clear that the new civilization must become very different from our present half-savage condition. The world is, as many people argue today, a madhouse, a place of unbalance and conflict. The new mentality, given the opportunity, should restore, or perhaps introduce for the first time since Eden, Essential sanity into our midst.

Chapter XX

THE INDIVIDUAL IN THE COMMUNITY

Society is made up of people, few of whom are in any degree self-conscious, aware of more than their personal desires. Those are still in a minority, who, to use Teilhard de Chardin's phrase, "know themselves as knowing" or, in David Stacton's words, "catch themselves experiencing experience." But, pursuing Stacton's idea, it is only then that they are capable of making use of experience in a positive and intelligent way. The very fact that they have achieved even a minor degree of detachment from inchoate mass mentality gives them an effective influence in the community which the ordinary, largely automatic mind has not. One person who thinks clearly and objectively is, from that angle, worth a hundred who drift with the tide, even if the best of the latter reach high office and seem to govern the State. For reforms and changes in the communal life take place first within the collective mental field and are then put into action by Cabinets and Parliaments whose acts are the last, not the first, in the chain of events.

The clear-minded individual is thus a force in the world, beneficent if his aim is toward the Essential, malefic if he uses his detachment for selfish ends. He may be charismatic if his inner development has gone far enough, and therefore his influence must of necessity be good. If he is only *mana,* his effectiveness will depend on which side he is: if on that of the shadow, he will do harm, if on the light side, good; but it is not by any means always obvious on which side he is. A reformer may be in the wider sense doing good, whereas the conservative may hold things back. The conservative-minded may also use his power in world affairs to stabilize and coordinate a change of pattern which would otherwise proceed too fast. He may therefore equally be on the side of light. The power of the objective thinker operates in various ways, is sometimes simply at the mental level. Sometimes, on the other hand, he may bring his ideas through into the physical and material area, where they may serve to bring about a new state of affairs.

At the mental level an individual mind may produce effects in two ways. First, just as the introduction of a new or increased quantity of a metal into an alloy affects the properties of that alloy, so does the presence in the community of a particular individual affect the over-all quality of the whole. But there is also a more active aspect of the matter, which is of a subtler nature and depends on the inter-relation between one individual and another at all levels. It is well known that every minute physical particle in some measure affects the whole universe. It has been said that a movement by a mouse on the surface of the earth affects the spin of the planet, which in turn affects the balance of the other planets and of the whole solar system, and spreads from there ever outward into space. In other words, there is no such thing as an independent entity in the universe, and what happens in one corner sends ripples indefinitely out from itself. The same thing applies at the mental level, but perhaps more forcefully. One can interpret the effect of mind on mind in terms of telepathy; the effect of a collective substratum of thinking may affect an individual mentality; but the fact remains that what I think and feel spreads all around and influences others. If I am *mana* or charismatic, and if I think clearly, the result is all the greater.

In India, where deep psychological facts are more explicitly expressed than perhaps anywhere else, the principle which takes people on pilgrimages to holy places or to the presence of holy people, is clearly laid down in the idea of what is called *darshana*. The idea is that, by contagion, as it were, people can be helped and spiritualized, receive a blessing which they would not get otherwise. It is as if some subtle power radiates from person, place, or revered object and evokes a response from another who has in himself a quality that enables him to respond to it. However much the principle becomes debased into a form of idolatry, it seems to have value in the community in general. The awakened person may, by the very fact of his presence in a group, influence the feeling of that group, whether or not he consciously knows it or tries to bring it about, because at a deep level we are all united and interdependent.

Another aspect of the matter can perhaps best be seen where works of art are concerned. There is much cant about the responsibility of the artist and his ability to elevate or deprave people. Yet when one discounts the nonsense, there is truth in the idea because what he produces serves as a focus for his inner mind, exhibiting and expressing what is there. As one painter remarked, what lies beyond you flows through your brush and into your work, whatever the subject of the painting may be. Technical skill though highly necessary then becomes secondary, because on it depends the ability of the artist to incarnate his ideas. Clearly, similar thoughts could come from a sculptor, a composer, a poet or any other creator of physical objects expressing subjective values. This would not apply to the technician or craftsman producing something like a colored photograph or a waxwork dummy, or merely reporting events in factual terms. It does apply to all forms of creative activity where the deeper levels of the mind are at play.

Although personal prejudice may be involved, art, which is the outcome of mental processes at a deeper level than that of normal consciousness, carries with it a quality which arises from the archetypal level. Whether it is — in the language used in this book — truly charismatic or whether it is only *mana* will depend on the individual who produces it. If it is the former, we have a work of art which is likely to endure. Roger Fry in one of his essays gave it as his opinion that the greater the work, the more often it can give a deep experience to the beholder, a peak experience, each time new and thrilling. This very adequate conclusion is borne out by the enduring quality of the great pictures, statues, music and other art forms.

On the other hand there is the form of "art" which may be novel, startling, confusing to the critics, but which is unlikely to last.

This may be the frenzied "abstract," the antithesis of the dead representational, whether produced by ape or man, or which may be merely the pathological outpouring of a sick mind (and there is much of that today). Critics seem to confuse a sick mind with a creative mind, and that not merely in the field of art. Its products, together with the kind of academic or popular art object are those to which Tillich refers by the telling German word *kitsch,* meaning approximately, "trash." He links it with the level at which religion loses its sense of ultimate values and becomes a social group with its own form of idolatry. The "sick" society of today may well actually be preparation for a new birth.

Between the two we have the objects which belong to the *mana* level. These can be in the wider sense good or bad: they may be of a nature which leads the mind toward the archetype itself, or of a kind which degrades and leads to a regressive movement in the individual. In any case, they are "exceptionally effective," as Jung puts it in defining the term *mana.* They may be said to radiate an influence, to have a power which, at this level, may belong either to the light or to the shadow aspect of an archetypal, polarized image, but not to the charismatic and Essential archetype itself.

This digression into the field of art seems the easiest way to illustrate yet again the general principle which applies to every department of life. We cannot exist without influencing those among whom we live. If we allow ourselves to be carried by mass feeling, by tradition and custom, without intelligently knowing what we are doing, we are apt to find ourselves involved through identification of our egos with this mass consciousness: we as individuals may be said to become submerged. Our task as human beings is to use the mind, first to consolidate, then to separate our egos from the mass, then to lift them clear of instinctive levels toward the true and archetypal Self which IS, however much it may also operate in the realm of *existence.*

The individual who has reached even the beginning of such a state is, then, *detached* in some degree from the mass, but he is not *isolated* from it. In fact, he finds himself much closer to it in his understanding. He is aware of his own identity with people, but he is not identified with them, a distinction which is highly important. For *identity* is *to be* another person or object, as the etymology tells us, whereas *identification* implies a "making an identity" (*id,* it; *ens,* being; *fio* or *facio,* make). The first IS, the latter involves a movement out from Self to not-self, the projection of a tentacle, as it were. Identity is of the nature of Being and depends on the feeling which is still and quiet; identification belongs to the emotional levels of the personal mind and tends to join things together, as thought tends to objectify and separate.

Along with this, identity is realized through the quiet Self; identification carries the personal ego with it and involves it in a situation where it may even for a time get lost. The negative aspect of identification, however, is isolation in a glass case or an ivory tower — which is also a coffin. It represents the conscious attempt of a person to withdraw from situations with which at the unconscious level he is in reality closely identified. The two poles co-exist there, whereas in *identity* there is no polarization. There is true objectivity. The one who is identified may have the quality of *mana,* but only the one who has moved from identification to conscious identity is charismatic in his own right, and so brings his fellows something of real and lasting value.

Chapter **XXI**

THE TASK OF THE INDIVIDUAL

If an individual develops a sense of Being, his daily life will alter, if only in that his values will change. This change does not happen all at once but bit by bit. He is likely to find that things which used to seem important lose their interest, while others — perhaps the "little things", in which, according to Evelyn Underhill, the Lord "comes" to men — acquire new significance and depth. For this to happen, however, one has to be willing to listen to the inner urges of the new type of consciousness which is seeking to emerge. The change has already taken place before it makes itself felt on the surface of daily life. It may begin as a result of cumulative peak experiences; it may be that at least something of it comes out as a result only of steady inner pressure.

If, at this stage, a person resists the new drive, he may become the victim of symptoms which are similar to those of ordinary neurosis; but these symptoms can never be resolved by psycho-analysis or by referring them "reductively" to early childhood. This is understandable because what is now causing conflict derives not from the past but from the future, the teleological or spiritual, archetypal root of each person's Being. Every man is himself basically a unique archetype, the image of which is reflected in his personality; his inner Self is projected into the polar world, in which we ordinarily dwell in the form of the personal ego. The latter is like a viceroy representing his sovereign, not himself the supreme ruler, though he sometimes tries to usurp the throne. Just as the image of an archetype has to carry with it the qualities of its source in the Essential world, so does this ego embody something of the sovereign's uniqueness and freewill — that of the basic man.

The ego is therefore capable of using this freewill, even in fighting against its own superior Root Self. This is what is meant by "estrangement," the "fall," and other similar terms which denote the fact that personal, existential man, until redeemed, is at odds with his deeper Self and with what he calls God. In the major world myths, we find always this theme, the hero becoming embroiled with the powers of darkness and evil; and then, through a form of death, he finds redemption and integration. Satan, also called Lucifer, the Light-Bringer, is in effect an image projected from the human mind. Natural instinct is neither good nor evil in itself. But if the human ego allows itself to be overwhelmed by instinct, it is apt to become inflated and to acquire personal characteristics which can be called Satanic. There are, fortunately rarely, people, especially in a psychotic society such as that of the Nazis, who are allied with what is, for man, the evil side of nature: evil not in itself, but because of the way man identifies with it, uses, and is then used by it. In most cases the natural and the Essential pulling, the one toward sub-human, mass consciousness, and the other toward higher individuality, cause strife in the personality. This conflict is projected outward by individuals and is seen in myth as the rival principles of God and Devil, Ahuramazda and Ahriman, and other warring characters or factions. In our own culture, it is noteworthy that Pan, the god of Nature, is depicted in much the same manner as later images of the horned and cloven-footed adversary of the existential image of God.

The man who is somewhere in Pope's "middle state" therefore is not cut off from himself but "estranged." There comes a time when this cannot continue. He sets out to become re-united to him-Self, to become cured of what is in effect the general disease of humanity, schizophrenia or split-mindedness. Indeed, it may be because of the acuteness of the conflict that so many psychotic schizophrenics are to be found among the sensitive, highly intelligent and awakened people in our midst. The basic condition has reached a critical point and, in too many cases, men have failed to take the steps which alone can bring about the integration of the two aspects of themselves, the personal and the Essential. So men suffer: they are not at ease with their fellows, with themselves, with life. Their symptoms are at once a sign that something is wrong and a goad to do something about the situation.

This point, moreover, tends to occur somewhere about the middle of a life which may, up to that time, have been lived adequately and comparatively happily. In the middle thirties (or between thirty and the mid-forties) there seems to be a time when most "breakdowns" occur, and are usually attributed to overwork and anxiety about becoming established in the world. These may indeed be factors, but there also seems much in Jung's suggestion that the first half of a life-span is spent in getting established in society and in the material world. Half way through, the awakened individual is called on — or rather, calls on himself — to become increasingly more philosophical and full of insight as his bodily strength wanes. He is, in a sense, preparing to die, to bring a certain chapter of his evolutionary history to a close. The numinous forces of his inner Being press on his personal life and endeavor to break the hold of daily routines and habits in order to replace them gradually by deeper vision. In India, this is the time when the family man enters the stage of *vanaprastha,* perhaps entering an *ashrama* or community under a *guru,* perhaps staying at home but living a more or less monastic life. This is the third phase of four *ashramas* (this same word being used also in this way). The first *ashrama* is that of the child and student, the second that of the family and business or professional man. The third phase is, or can be, succeeded by the last *ashrama* or stage, that of *sannyasa,* when a man returns to give to the world what he has discovered.

In the west these stages are not distinguished, but they can be found in the lives of many people, often overlapping to such an extent that they cause disharmony between the inner need and the outer life. The psychiatrist (especially in America) sometimes the priest, then becomes the *guru* or teacher. Some people fall into the hands of groups and societies which dispense initiations and supposed spiritual ranks, adopt creeds set out, it is said, by a hidden but quasi-divine teacher through his chosen mouthpiece. In any case, the background drive in the disciple is the same, and emanates from within the individual, urging him to try to find more light on the meaning of life. This impulse

140

persists from then on, so that even if somebody starts down what is bound to be a blind alley, it does not matter so much as that he begins to move. If one joins with a narrow sectarian group, or a distorted teaching, he will find himself sooner or later self-hounded out of his false securities, his idols will show feet of clay, and he will be driven to continue his search elsewhere. There is no more relentless Pursuer than the Hound of Heaven, as Francis Thompson (himself markedly schizoid) well knew.

The exact and best path for any individual can only be determined by himself. There are old observances and disciplines which suggest general lines of approach to Truth, and these can serve, if only for a time. There are also many people who set themselves up as teachers of those they believe to be less enlightened than themselves. They too may have something to offer — for a time. But the Gospels warn us against "false prophets," especially at "the end of the age", a time which we may well feel to be the present day. True, to come into the presence of a genuinely charismatic individual or to visit a place where centuries of worship have built up a certain atmosphere may evoke something very much worth while in an individual; but ultimately *he is the only arbiter, he is his only Master,* and becomes increasingly so as he deepens in understanding and awareness.

At the same time, it has to be understood that nobody else can, or should try to coerce another into starting on the way, whether by threats, as in some primitive churches, or by promise of reward. Religion — for such it is — *must be embraced voluntarily because of a realized need,* not by lip service only; and then it does not matter what external form that religion takes.

If one is at the point where it is right that he should make a real start in the direction of "return," he finds himself in a dilemma. For to adopt such a course one has to be willing to pay a price, no less than to be prepared to give up old habits, attitudes, perhaps even material possessions. This is demanded of one by one's Self, and to refuse produces difficulties of all kinds, from which, as they are self-projected, there can be no escape until they are resolved intelligently and consciously. If one has "seen God," as they say in the East, he cannot turn his back with impunity. Peeping Toms are not allowed in the Essential world.

To find exactly what to do is the task of each individual. He may temperamentally turn first to one kind of discipline or to another; he may find ritual and external observances of real value; he may become more introverted and meditative. At a later stage he may discover that imposed rules and ceremonies have become a habit or a compulsion and in reality impede further discovery; but to live the life of a hermit may equally be an attempt to escape from ordinary life. Indeed, it is natural that — allowing for the unstable and changeable individual who will always exist among us — alternation between two aspects is a normal course of events. We normally move from a *yin* phase onto a *yang* one as time unwinds itself through our lives, and part of our task is to be aware when the moment has come to change over.

Another aspect of man's quest is to awaken. Ouspensky, inspired by Gurdjieff, tells us that most of the time when we are "awake" and going about our ordinary daily tasks, we are in reality almost as unconscious as when we are in bed at night. Yet notwithstanding this, we can live an ordinary life, act with intelligence. We find the difference, however, when we make the mental effort of recollecting ourselves and becoming aware of where we are and what we are doing.

This old Buddhist practice, more recently advocated by the two Russians just mentioned, is very simple to carry out, at any moment, even in the middle of some activity. It consists simply in centering one's attention and then watching oneself in the field of action, whether this be physical or mental. In doing this one sees the little self — the ego — in its context, and many things come into relief. On one occasion a group was having tea in a large cafe and discussing this very matter. Those present tried the process as an experiment, with the result that many things previously unnoticed came into view: the sound of the band, the noise of talk and crockery, the smell of food, even the taste of what one was eating, while one became aware of each separate personality in the group. Gradually, however, these once more faded into the background as the discussion went on.

A French psychologist, Dr. Artus, used to get people to close their eyes and recollect themselves, then to open them and *look* from the still point inside them. They were told not to think of color, form, the nature of what was seen, but simply to use vision in pure form. The results were interesting and showed also the difficulty of keeping up the process of poised observation; for after a matter of seconds, most people found their minds beginning to oscillate, to think, feel, name, and so on. In the same way, to try to visualize a circle and follow it mentally round the whole circumference was a most difficult exercise in practice. Most people got lost after only a little way. Similar things can, of course, be done using any of the senses.

Persistence in self-recollection or self-remembering, simple as it is, proves effective in changing one's focus of attention. Gradually, it is found that an individual learns much both about himself and also about his environment at any given time. One sees himself in context. There is, however, one proviso, which seems to be often overlooked in the groups which advocate this method. It is not sufficient to become aware of oneself in the physical environment, and outward turned. One should also come to the point of discovering what goes on alongside the place of focused consciousness, how perhaps one reaches automatically for the packet of cigarettes, takes one and lights it without even being aware of doing so. Then also one may be thinking of something, or performing some task which does not require full attention, while another part of him is off down the "labyrinthine ways of his own mind," following the tracks of what the Freudian calls "free association." This leads into the unconscious, and to some stressed complex of thought and feeling. It does not happen without reason, and, inevitably, conscious pursuit of the road leads to discovery of something about oneself previously hidden. The need therefore is not only to learn to become aware of the *external* world and of the ego at the center of its particular horizon, but also to observe with the same objectivity this same ego at work *subjectively,* within its own inner field, the unconscious. If this subjective analysis is left out in practices which increase awareness of the objective world, it is too often found that while a certain clarity and power of physical consciousness develops, an individual remains with his neurotic traits untouched and alongside the field of his awareness. The result is apt to show in a form of arrogant egoism and a sense of superiority which is unpleasant, unhealthy and perhaps even dangerous.

Fundamentally, however, the very simple exercise of trying to awake and to remain awake for any length of time, is very easy — too easy and simple, in fact for us to carry it on without much practice. We are in the habit of *doing,* and this is learning to *not-do* as also, probably, to *un-do* in the usual sense of loosening up knots and tight places in our minds.

It also means that the point from which one observes, and which is still *I,* cannot be the active ego itself. One cannot see things happening when one is entirely involved in the event. The old tag about the wood and the trees applies. To see the wood as a whole one must be outside or above it. So, to observe the lower form of selfhood at work one must, even in some small degree, have detached oneself from it while, at the same time, since it is "I" which is watching "me," there is a clear link between the two; otherwise it would be a matter of watching somebody else, another ego, and not oneself in any situation. The ego would be split, as one finds in severe neurosis and especially in schizophrenic psychosis. It follows that the observer must be on a higher rung of the ladder of consciousness, and hence a step nearer to the level of Being than the self being observed.

Gradually, this state of suspended observation can become something approaching normal for any individual who persistently practices it. He begins to find himself oriented more or less permanently towards the Pole Star of his deeper and essential Self, and sets his course through life accordingly. Inevitably, however, he will at times lose his bearings, yaw off course, as he is caught by waves and currents in the world around him; but once he has his point of reference, he will gradually find it easier to return to it when the stressful moment has gone by.

This does not mean any very great exaltation in consciousness of the kind which one occasionally meets in rare and truly charismatic people. It is something which the individual can begin to work for at any time. Presumably the real saint (not necessarily to be found in the official list) or Arhat, or liberated man, would be one who dwelt permanently at the level of Being, "face to face with God," one whose whole personal and existential life was planned and patterned from that point. To become such a person seems to be the ultimate destiny of each one of us: individuals in the truest and deepest sense, and ready to pass on into superhumanity. This is the tradition in every religious system, though we cannot know it for ourselves until eventually we reach a much higher level of Essential awareness than the glimpse we have today. But we can make a start in doing what amounts to a movement which, instead of sliding along the time track with the present moment, consists in effect in rising from that present, in a "vertical" direction from the moment toward another level of our total Being. Teilhard de Chardin speaks of individuals whose focus has moved on into what he calls the "noosphere," the consciousness of the future. It may well be assumed that these are the ones of whom we are now speaking. Nor does it mean that one becomes so spiritual that one loses touch with personal life and needs. On the contrary, in a sense it means that the individual is more fully incarnate in the physical world than ever. The truly spiritualized person lives "from heaven above *and earth beneath*." The ladder of evolution and self-realization may have its head in the heavens, but it needs its foot well placed on the earth, else it may tip over. There is a saying in occultism that "the Way is strewn with wrecks." But the wreckage is due to a misconception as to the nature of that Way, which we will now attempt to discuss.

Chaper XXII

ONE WORLD

At the end of the last chapter we said we would *attempt* to discuss the misconception which is likely to frustrate, if it does not wreck, the one who is trying to find his way to Truth. The word is used because in our present state and frame of mind (again, the word *frame* is significant because we work within limits when we operate at the discursive and linguistic levels) we cannot speak in a reasonable way about a world view which extends, it seems, indefinitely beyond any frame. It is a vista of what we may call a "Beyond-world," one which may be *imagined* as yet rather than actually observed; but this world is not merely imaginary or fantastic. It is a very real world, one which is there — very much there, even though we may not know of its existence — and not a place of dreams.

Imagination can help us to develop true vision in that it can be used as a means of obtaining answers to one's questions. A question carefully formulated contains its own answer latent within it. Hence it can and will take us from one place to another in our mind. If one says to himself, "I wonder what happens when . . . ?" and then sets to work to try to imagine an answer, it is surprising how, after a period of mental weaving, of trial and error, a true solution often appears. Fantasy, however, is a circular movement leading nowhere except to the personal ego round which it centers. It represents emotional and wishful thinking. The distinction is important and needs to be discovered for oneself. Fantasy takes one deeper into the realm of *maya* or illusion. Imagination points toward reality. Much of the work done by people in what should be an attempt to find enlightenment is in fact to build up a fantastic carapace of ideas and feelings where the ego is the central element and derives satisfaction for itself. The cause is our confusion between creative imagination and fantasy, which mimics it. If this were not so, many a self-styled teacher of spiritual matters would find himself out of work, with no pupils, because they would see that to promise rapid development and spiritual preferment was merely to indulge the personal ego and not to touch the deeper Self.

On the other hand, the austerity of the real search is quite another matter, for it demands nothing less than stripping off everything which stands between oneself and Reality; and that means the personal self and its demands have to be left behind until, eventually, true Self-hood stands naked before one in all its glory. In *The Bhagavad-Gita* there is a magnificent section where the disciple, Arjuna, asks God, his true Essence in the form of Krishna, to show Himself as he *is*, unveiled. This Krishna does, and the revelation is almost too much for Arjuna. In the same way the vision of the Christ was too much for Saul of Tarsus before he became Paul.

Always, until the final illumination, man, as ultimate Self, is veiled, more or less hidden. The pure vision would overwhelm the person not yet ready for it. But the veils do more than conceal; they are also the instruments by which this supreme Self works in the field of the manifested, evolving universe.

If we now consider the men and women of our time, as we know them, it is very evident that they are incomplete. Their field is limited, their mental activities restricted to the mechanisms of their bodies and the mind behind the body. They are *personae* or masks. In particular, the intrinsic mind appears to operate above a "floor," the partition between waking and sleeping life, perhaps also between physical life and what we call death. There is a suggestion, somewhere in the voluminous writings of H. P. Blavatsky, which is interesting in this connection. It is derived from Eastern sources and suggests that the inner and Essential man had adopted or adapted the animal body and its instinctive life to his own ends, but that this body is no more a part of himself than is the vehicle

147

he drives. He is in close contact with it but while it acts like the weight of a pendulum, regulating his activities, serving as a fulcrum against which he himself, as mind, can press, as well as a meeting place between himself and the self-existent physical world, he is not really a denizen in this world. His feet must rest on it but he must neither hover above it nor be rooted even ankle-deep in it.

If this is true, it indicates why our relationship to the material world is different from what we call the mental realm, or what occultists term the "astral plane." Physical objects are outside ourselves as personalities, mental "objects" are not, or are not realized as such by most people. This very situation suggests the great value of the physical world for our mental growth, for it enables us to develop powers in the mind, and particularly the detached objectivity we call scientific. This objectivity starts as regards the physical realm, but, once acquired, it is capable of being carried inward in self-examination. Without the material world, such a quality would be much more difficult to develop, if it were possible at all. In the reciprocal direction, action as against perception, we also have in the physical world a realm where we can work controlledly on objects, watch the result, and so discover new ways of doing things, re-arranging and so creating without ourselves being involved in the changes taking place. This world, the earth, is hence of inestimable value to mankind even if it is not our intrinsic possession but only a place where we can play and work and exercise our inner selves.

Just as the foregoing suggests that personal man operates from above a "floor" which lies between him and the physical earth-level, it seems clear that there is also a ceiling to this personality. Here, as in the dome of an observatory, a window sometimes opens to give a glimpse of another sphere, the Numinous or Spiritual. This dome then closes, leaving perhaps an open chink which represents the permanent influence of what has been seen. Beyond the ceiling, we now feel, is another world, quite different from the personal one, yet one in which we ourselves live or ARE in a trans-personal form. The impulses which enter the personal field are in some way similar to those which come in from the sensory, material "end," with, however, the difference of quality we discussed in another chapter. This difference, in brief, is a *total* complementariness which excludes *nothing* whatever, even the differences we notice.

148

So *personal* man lives between two worlds, the physical and the Spiritual, or so it seems as he makes his mental "construct" of the situation. This is done at the level of the polarized ordinary mind, in the realm of *maya,* so can only be taken as image or analogy, not as the real state of affairs.

There is light to be gained from the Indian Vedantic philosophy where it specifies just what are the "veils" over the basic Self or *Atman.* Vedanta is a multiple system with many overlaps, and it can lead one into hopeless confusion. But in all cases, whether the "veils" be called *koshas, upadhis* or *shariras,* representing divisions such as those between that which thinks, that which feels emotion, that where feeling is quiet bliss, it seems that mind retains its place as the central principle. The word *manas* may be taken to represent pure, unconditioned mind, inactive in its own nature but becoming active when energized either by *kama,* instinct, desire or emotion, on the one hand, or Buddhi, the spiritual and essential aspect of feeling on the other. Let it be said that the use of the word *manas* for this purpose will not please all scholars, because in some systems *manas* is said to be only an attribute of a central principle, *antahkarana.* This, however, represents more of a linear axis running throughout the total man than a point within him. But for our purposes, apart from its convenience, the concept of *manas* as the center of the circle of existence is of most use.

Manas may be said to lie at the junction between what our mental image presents to us as the personal, and the Essential, straddling the two as it becomes active, and extended on either or both sides through the general feeling function. As we have already suggested, feeling is experienced in dual form, the one, emotion, linked with instinct, the other at the Numinous level which we only dimly understand and which in Vedanta is called *buddhi.*

Two further philosophical considerations have to be mentioned if we want to amplify our picture. One is that, again in Vedanta, there is a distinction between the *rupa,* form or dimensional levels of the universe, and the *arupa* or formless, non-extended ones. The former are more or less material, the latter spiritual and non-material. The latter are usually depicted as superior to the first, and placed as steps from the densest matter, gradually becoming less dense until — and here is the crux —

149

they suddenly cease to be material and become dimensionless, a mathematical point. This is at the level where we have placed *manas,* pure Mind, one aspect of which would therefore project itself into the dimensional material world or worlds, the other into the space-timeless spiritual world, or, if Vedanta is correct, worlds.

Such a scheme gives us a picture in which progressive conciousness would work step by step from physical sensation toward *manas,* through it, and on toward the summit of the total human field. Here supreme Spirit, known in the East as *Atman,* and equated with God Himself, stands at the head of the ladder.

There is however, another way of considering things, which rests on the fact that our word *man* is known to be related to the Sanskrit word *manas.* Man is the entity which operates through *manas,* on this planet at least. Hence, *manas* is the very center of his whole field as man.

What then of the "superior" or *arupa* spiritual aspect of himself? It seems reasonable to propose a different picture from the staircase idea by placing the *arupa,* formless, dimensionless essence of man in another dimension. *Manas* would be the center of the field of existence for man, and the formless, non-dimensional principle or principles could then be thought of as on an axis at right angles to the plane of the personality. This axis impinges on the personal or *rupa* self through the center, *manas,* and when it spreads its influence into the personal field, it does so through pure Mind. This is a variation of the picture in an earlier chapter where we emphasize the dimensionlessness experienced at peak moments as we enter the realm of the Numinous.

That this is not a new and heretical attitude is to be seen from a number of ancient writings which present what seems to be the purest form of Buddhism. Notably there is the "Huang Po Doctrine of Universal Mind," as explained in a booklet issued by the Buddhist Society of London. In this, it seems, the term *mind* is used to represent an absolute, transcendental function, and not only the center of the personal man. It incorporates the totality of Essence at the same time as it focuses human life round itself.

Here an analogy may serve. It is, like the whole of this discussion, derived from the discursive pattern of the personal levels, hence it is real only in the sense that *maya* reflects Reality; but it is the only way in which we can make plain the point in this chapter.

150

If a sailor is in the middle of a sea which extends all around him, he will be surrounded by a circle, the horizon. *He is the center of his world.* Whichever way he looks, he sees water over-reached by a hemisphere of sky which he knows is not "real" but only an illusion caused by his mind and the limited sense of sight. There is no question of moving from left side to right and seeing something new and different. He remains at the center. On the other hand, if he rises from where he stands, his horizon widens, and yet, even if he sees a distant coast or another ship, he is still at the center. We will call this center the *manasic* principle. Rising vertically his awareness expands but it shows him the same sea, possibly with land in it, extending all around. In other words, spiritual progress cannot occur along a horizontal (or, to be exact, slightly curved) plane. The individual, discursive mind needs to focus at the central point, *mana*s, and to move off in an entirely new dimension from there.

There is a light-hearted song which can be used as a parable. In its briefest form it says,

> A bear went over a mountain
> And what do you think he saw?
> Why! The other side of the mountain,
> That is what he saw.

An intelligent human being would have stopped on the top of the mountain so that he could see both sides at once. A bear, however, symbol of the human being acting instinctively rather than with conscious intelligence, thinks he is acquiring new vision by going past the place which matters, and finds himself in precisely the same state as before, on "the other side of the mountain." It is on the peak alone that a transformation of understanding can take place.

This transformation shows us the *maya* or unreality in which we live our daily lives, the lack of comprehension which arises from polarized thinking, which places matter at one end of a line, spirit at the other. From the focus of pure *manas* we learn otherwise because we see the whole horizon, its diameter extended perhaps indefinitely, as a circle within which we can travel endlessly without escape. But Truth can only be found in a different way, based on the look-out point which we discover as we clear our minds entirely and utterly of all attachment and conditioning. We then learn that the circumference, already spoken of in terms of the Ouroboros, or snake with its tail in its mouth, does not consist of one half which is spiritual, good, light, the other material, evil, dark, but that there is only one circle, uniform all through. It is we, with our imperfect, discursive minds, who invent a division and label one side Spirit, the other matter. The world of existence is only dual in our conception of it. In Reality there is but one World. If, with our minds, we look in one direction we label it Spiritual, if in the other, material, with all the qualities we think are connected with these terms. Moreòver, if the highest Spiritual level and the deepest material aspects of our illusory picture seem to place them at extreme opposites and as being outside what we call ourselves, the densest physical and the highest and most transcendental are one and the same. *One is not superior or higher than the other, both are equally Good.* Opposites meet at infinity, that is, at the level of Essence. There is only one Infinity. *The world of our daily life IS the spiritual world,* though our mental habit shows them to us as different and even antagonistic. It we understand this, much falls into place both in our mental pictures and also in our daily lives. The contradictions of the discursive mind are integrated in the Essential mind. There are not two worlds, the one Spiritual, the other material. There is only WORLD. There are not animal man and divine man. There is only MAN.

We shall also see the force of a tradition that sainthood, perfection, liberation, enlightenment can only be reached while incarnate in a physical body. Hence the value of learning to *live* what we know, and the insistence on this in the Buddhist Eightfold Path, as in the Christian and other faiths. In active life, to do what is in the widest sense right at every and any moment of the day or night is the way to become truly spiritual. We should not try to escape from the thing which lies before us, the immediate task needing to be done, in search of "higher" things. Whatever conditions may have been in the remote past, the yogi or holy man of today has to learn to perform his yoga in the midst of ordinary life, not to "take sannyasa," away from this. Some wise Hindus, judges and others, realize this and carry on their offices, changing only their private and personal behavior.

A wise Brahmin was once asked "How do I find my true mission in life?" He rather caustically replied, "Why do you want a mission? To feel important? Your mission in life is to do whatever duty is in front of you, however humble. After that a new duty will arise, and another. That is your mission."

T. S. Eliot sums up the whole matter in "Little Gidding" when he says,

> . . . And the end of our exploring
> Will be to arrive where we started
> And to know it for the first time.

Our task is to become aware; for in this, which is essentially a process of freeing the mind from the things which hamper it, is the true way to achievement of the perfection which leads out from humanity into a further State beyond our vision today. What better place is there to work in than in daily contact with others?

This, however, can only be learned when we reach the poised state where our awareness is suspended between action and non-action, where all things are equal and not classified according to our likes and dislikes, our past conditioning or our future hopes. *Nihil humanum a me alienum puto*, "I consider nothing human alien to myself," said Terence. He might have gone further and omitted the word *human* so that the whole creation would be included. This would give his saying wider meaning. Paul Tillich puts the matter in other terms: " . . . in man nothing is merely biological as nothing is merely spiritual. Every cell in his body participates in his freedom and spirituality, and every act of his spiritual creativity is nourished by his vital dynamics."

Put in other terms, this means that we should reject no part of ourselves, psychological or physical, however seemingly repugnant. Our body and our instincts are as necessary to complete integration as is the Spiritual principle. The physical needs of the body not only require fulfillment, but feeling should be used and experienced to the full. The power to enjoy things, and its opposite, the power to feel pain and suffering are both parts of personal life. Neither should be rejected. But the awakened person does not let himself become involved and carried away by them, as this causes regression as far as his sense of identity is concerned.

That self should always be learning through its experience and becoming at once stronger and different in quality from that of the instinct-driven man. It is the observer of what takes place, and the less resistance or involvement there is in any situation, the better.

Obviously enough it is easy — unless one is hag-ridden by super-egoic false morality — to enjoy pleasurable experiences. The danger is to lose insight into what one is doing, thereby harming oneself and perhaps others. It is less easy to keep the same attitude toward pain, physical or mental; the natural instinct is to avoid it. Yet if it is accepted without resistance, not only does the actual pain seem to be less, it becomes a constructive experience. One of the present writers remembers having a painful tooth drilled. He naturally flinched until he tried the experiment of drawing himself mentally back from the situation. Instead of trying to forget it and think about something else, however, he found that he was able, as it were, to turn round and let himself feel the drill and the pain it was causing. It became a fascinating experience. Then his detachment would slip for a moment and he was back again, reacting and flinching. But each time he was able once more to free himself, the positive, constructive aspect returned. At the end, he was very tired, but nevertheless he had learned something, and found the principle of it applicable in every other phase of life. He had not dissociated himself as happens naturally in hysterical temperaments, or artificially as when a person is hypnotized, but the withdrawal had taken the form of a conscious and objective mental action, and that made all the difference.

This is an important point. The need for deliberate, conscious action shows us something applicable to the modern tendency to seek freedom by "permissiveness." Merely to let oneself go, to yield to one's impulses is one thing. To use intelligence and to know what one is doing and why, is another. The first is an undisciplined and regressive state, the latter, based on self-knowledge, however partial, represents not aimless wandering but positive exploration of oneself, following a discipline which is healthy because self-directed and purposeful. The Self which does the directing is of a higher order than the merely personal ego, center of the instinct-built mind. Even if it has not yet reached the level of the Essential, and if it is operating in the material field, it is nevertheless nearer to the center than the ordinary ego.

To sum up, the way to spiritual enlightenment is not away from the material world but, on the contrary, intelligently and consciously into it. The enlightened Man is more fully incarnate than the unaware, not less so. His personality — and this is the reverse of the false idea of "killing out the personal" — is stronger, not weaker, than that of the ordinary person, because his complete spiritual and material sides combine to give him their life and power. This occurs as he learns increasingly to operate from the center of himself, the still place which is pure, free Mind. The one who has even momentarily succeeded in doing this finds that, step by step, his universe becomes ordered and integrated. He discovers this both within and without. He himself becomes individual and united, and this harmony is reflected in the external world despite its seeming discords and disparities. Moreover there grows in him the sense that what he calls *within* is also *without*: he and the universe he lives in are in Reality and in Essence one.

EPILOGUE

In the course of this book our endeavor has been, first to show the vital importance of the mind of man, not only to himself but to the whole planet, at every level. What he does or refrains from doing will determine the fate of the Earth.

The second point has been to try to show the need today for progressive change and reorganization of our world outlook. This outlook ranges from the minority who have deep insight — not of necessity to be found among intellectuals, scientists, theologians or philosophers — to the simplest, primitive peasant. But it is no less the collective than the individual which counts, even though reactionary forces, both in science and in communism, tend to consider him only as a digit in a statistical framework. The crude idea we call democracy is a first step in the right direction, however much our political and social institutions may limp and creak.

Third, we have tried to indicate the signs of incipient change, the challenge to authority and tradition, the demand for freedom from the past, and permission for each person to choose his way of life, however much of a mess he may make of it: these things, if not carried too far, are all hopeful; while on a more constructive note, the widespread move toward a positive existential attitude, and the focus on the vital present moment, all point to what seems required.

In with all this we have argued that each man is his own master, the arbiter of his fate. Only he can change himself. If he images the Christ, the Buddha, a saint or master as his redeemer, these images reflect his own Self — even if there are, in fact

156

Personages of superhuman stature, as seems probable, and as is believed in all esoteric and true religions. Only by his own acts can man enter the world of mind renewed. There are no short-cuts, whether by disciplines or anti-disciplines, by drugs, or in any other way than by *deliberately sought awareness.* True, we can learn much by holding on to the hand of the ancient intuitive tradition of real Religion purified of its idolatry. But we have also said that a time comes when child-man must be ready to let go of that hand and stand alone. That time is, for many an awakened person, now.

Needless to say, we repudiate the blasphemy that man is by nature a sinner in need of forgiveness from an all-too-manlike god. Ignorant and unconscious he may be; but is a child a sinner simply because he is not yet an adult? On the contrary, there runs through all these essays a great respect for man. Shabby, mediocre as he is, his potential is immense. His outlook may be stunted, distorted, he is still on the defensive and feels the need to protect himself both physically and mentally; so he shuts himself in with prejudice and intolerance. But when his discoveries go far enough he finds the liberating secret of true invulnerability in becoming utterly defenseless. A bullet shatters a pane of glass because the glass resists. The bullet causes only a ripple in air but leaves no scar. In a vacuum it causes no disturbance at all. So with our minds. If we can learn to understand the universe from within, to feel our unity with it, we shall no longer need the instinctive reactions of fear or aggression, and the whole face of civilization will change.

We are inclined to be dismayed and afraid of what is going on around us today. Jeremiahs and Cassandras prophesying doom abound. But we feel that if the present is properly understood, though we are in very great danger, there is also much ground for hope. It will depend on how intelligently we, as human minds, using all the functions of thought, feeling and the impulse to act, learn to cooperate with the universal Mind out of which we and the whole of creation were made.

We have the means to do this; we have the guide lines to start us off. If we can see them and make use of them as we should. the future is secure. The choice is ours.

BIBLIOGRAPHY

The *Bhagavad-Gita*. Various translations.

The *Holy Bible*.

The *I Ching* or *Book of Changes,* edited by J. Blofeld, Dutton, New York, N. Y., 1965; Cary F. Baynes translation, Bollingen Foundation, Princeton University Press, Princeton, N. J., 1967.

Allen, H. Warner   *The Timeless Moment,* Faber & Faber, Ltd., London, 1946.

Bendit, L. J.   *The Mirror of Life and Death,* Theosophical Publishing House, Adyar, India, 1965; Quest Books, Theosophical Publishing House, Wheaton, Illinois, 1967.

Self-Knowledge: A Yoga for the West, Quest Books, Theosophical Publishing House,Wheaton, Illinois, 1967.

Bucke, R. M.   *Cosmic Consciousness,* Dutton, New York, 1929.

Blavatsky, H. P.   *The Stanzas of Dzyan,* Theosophical Publishing Society, London, 1909.

The Secret Doctrine, Theosophical Publishing House, Adyar, India, 1961.

Challoner, H. K. and Northover, R.   *Out of Chaos,* The Theosophical Publishing House, London, 1967.

Coster, G.   *Psycho-Analysis for Normal People,* Oxford University Press, London, 1947.

Yoga and Western Psychology, Oxford University Press, London,1947.

Dunne, J. W.   *An Experiment with Time,* Faber & Faber, Ltd., London, 1948.

Evans-Wentz, D. Y.   *The Tibetan Book of the Dead,* Oxford University Press (paperback), London, 1968.

158

Fausset, Hugh l'A.	*The Flame and the Light,* Abelard-Schuman, London, 1958.
	The Lost Dimension, Stuart & Watkins, London, 1966.
Freud, Sigmund	*The Interpretation of Dreams,* Avon (paperback), New York, 1965; Basic Books (hard), New York, 1955.
	Psychopathology of Everyday Life, Norton (hard and paperback), New York, 1965.
Holroyd, S.	*Emergence from Chaos,* Hillary, New York, 1957.
Howe, E. Graham and Le Mesurier, L.	*The Open Way,* Methuen, London, 1950.
Huxley, Aldous	*Doors of Perception and Heaven and Hell,* Harper's (hard and paperback), New York, 1964.
	The Perennial Philosophy, Harper's (hardback), New York, 1945; Meridian (paperback), World Publishing Co., Cleveland, Ohio, 1945.
Jacobi, J.	*The Psychology of Jung,* Yale University Press, New Haven, Conn., 1943.
James, William	*Varieties of Religious Experience,* Longmans Green, New York, 1905.
Johnson, Raynor	*The Imprisoned Splendour,* Hodder & Stoughton, London, 1954.
	Nurslings of Immortality, Harper's, New York, 1957.
	Watcher on the Hills, Harper's, New York, 1965.
Jung, C. G.	*Collected Works,* Routledge & Kegan Paul, London; Bollingen Foundation, New York.
Krishnamurti, J.	*Writing and Reports of Talks,* Gollancz, London; Krishnamurti Writings, Ojai, California; Quest Books, Theosophical Publishing House, Wheaton, Illinois.
Lao Tse	*The Tao Teh King* (various translations)

Martin, P. W.	*Experiment in Depth,* Routledge & Kegan Paul, London, 1955.
Maslow, A.	*Towards a Psychology of Being,* Van Nostrand (paperback), Princeton, N. J., 1962.
Merton, Thomas	*The Way of Chuang Tzu,* New Directions (paperback), New York, 1965.
Osborn, Arthur W.	*The Expansion of Awareness,* Theosophical Publishing House, Adyar, India; Quest Books, Theosophical Publishing House, Wheaton, Illinois, 1961.
Ouspensky, P. D.	*In Search of the Miraculous,* Harcourt & Brace, New York, 1949.
Payne, P. D. and Bendit, L. J.	*The Psychic Sense,* Faber & Faber, London, 1943; Quest Books, Theosophical Publishing House, Wheaton, Illinois, 1967.
Progoff, Ira	*The Symbolic and the Real,* Julian Press, New York, 1943.
Tillich, Paul	Works (21 titles), several publishers.
Vyvyan, J.	*The Case Against Jones,* James Clarke, London, 1966.
Watts, Alan	*Myth and Ritual in Christianity,* Vanguard, New York, 1954.
	The Wisdom of Insecurity, Pantheon, New York, 1949.
Wickes, Frances	*The Inner World of Childhood,* Appleton, New York, N. Y., 1966; Meredith, New York, 1966.
	The Inner World of Man, Unger, New York, 1959.
Wilson, Colin	*Introduction to the New Existentialism,* Hutchinson, London, 1966; Houghton (paperback), Boston, 1966.

QUEST BOOKS

are published by
The Theosophical Society in America,
a branch of a world organization
dedicated to the promotion of brotherhood and
the encouragement of the study of religion,
philosophy, and science to the end that man may
better understand himself and his place in
the universe. The Society stands for complete
freedom of individual search and belief.
In the Theosophical Classics Series
well-known occult works are made
available in popular editions.

We invite you to read these Quest books:

THE EXPANSION OF AWARENESS
By Arthur W. Osborn
272 pages of psychological and parapsychological wisdom
from a distinguished author, intellectual-mystic.

THE REALITY ILLUSION
By Ralph Strauch
How we create the world we experience.
What we "see" out there is not necessarily so.

CULTURE, CRISIS AND CREATIVITY
By Dane Rudhyar
Does our culture have a future? Rudhyar, famous
astrologer, occult-philosopher, offers a powerful
indictment of our tendency to "follow the crowd."

EVOLUTION OF INTEGRAL CONSCIOUSNESS
By Haridas Chaudhuri
Consciousness as a holistic, interdependent phenomenom
that permeates all of our activities, physical,
emotional, mental, and spiritual.

SPECTRUM OF CONSCIOUSNESS
By Ken Wilber
An added dimensional view of psycho-therapies; the non-
duality of spirit; the essential unity of all religions.

Available from:
The Theosophical Publishing House
306 West Geneva Road
Wheaton, Illinois 60189